IMAGES
of America

UNITARIANS AND UNIVERSALISTS OF WASHINGTON, D.C.

Muriel Davies welcomes a child to River Road Unitarian Church (later renamed the River Road Unitarian Universalist Congregation) in Bethesda, Maryland. River Road was one of the congregations formed through an initiative from All Souls Church and its minister, A. Powell Davies. After her husband's death in 1957, Muriel became the congregation's first administrator and religious education director. (River Road Unitarian Universalist Congregation.)

ON THE COVER: The children of All Souls Church, Unitarian, are posed here in June 1929. This photograph was taken on the front steps of the congregation's third and current building on Harvard Street in northwest Washington, D.C. (All Souls Church, Unitarian.)

IMAGES
of America

UNITARIANS AND UNIVERSALISTS OF WASHINGTON, D.C.

Bruce T. Marshall

ARCADIA
PUBLISHING

Published by Arcadia Publishing
Charleston SC, Chicago IL, Portsmouth NH, San Francisco CA

Library of Congress Control Number: 2009930979

For all general information contact Arcadia Publishing at:
Telephone 843-853-2070
Fax 843-853-0044
E-mail sales@arcadiapublishing.com
For customer service and orders:
Toll-Free 1-888-313-2665

Visit us on the Internet at www.arcadiapublishing.com

For church historians, who labor in attics, closets, and basements to keep the stories of their congregations alive.

CONTENTS

ACKNOWLEDGMENTS

Many people have contributed to the formation of this book. I appreciate the interest shown in this project and the willing assistance I received.

I would like to thank Molly Freeman and the wonderful Archives Committee at All Souls Church, Unitarian, in Washington, D.C. Their prior work and careful record keeping made this book possible. I would also like to thank the Reverend Lillie Henley and Marguerite Bogle at the Universalist National Memorial Church in Washington, D.C., John Hurley and Sabe Graham at the Unitarian Universalist Association in Boston, Frances O'Donnell and Jessica Suarez at the Andover-Harvard Theological Library in Cambridge, and the Reverend Amanda Poppei at the Washington Ethical Society in Washington, D.C. All these people gave valuable assistance and direction in locating the images used in this book. I am also grateful to the following people who shared their insights: the Reverend Roger Fritts of Cedar Lane Unitarian Universalist Church, the Reverend John Manwell at Paint Branch Unitarian Universalist Church, and the Reverend Bill Gardiner. I would also like to thank the many other representatives of Washington-area Unitarian Universalist congregations who have so graciously allowed access to their archives. Finally I would like to thank my editors at Arcadia Publishing: Brooksi Hudson, who encouraged me to take on this project, and Elizabeth Bray, who patiently guided me through the process.

The sources of the photographs in this book are as follows (unless otherwise noted): All Souls Church, Unitarian (ASC); Universalist National Memorial Church (UNMC); Unitarian Universalist Association archives (UUA); Andover-Harvard Theological Library, Harvard Divinity School, Harvard University (AHTL); Cedar Lane Unitarian Universalist Church (CLUUC); Unitarian Universalist Congregation of Fairfax (UUCF); Washington Ethical Society (WES); Davies Memorial Unitarian Universalist Church (DMUUC); and River Road Unitarian Universalist Congregation (RRUUC).

I would like to express special thanks to my wife, Amy Dibner, who has been encouraging and supportive of this endeavor from the start.

INTRODUCTION

Creating a congregation and sustaining it throughout years and generations is an expression of hope. It is a statement that the values under which this community have gathered matter and that its account of what humanity is called to do and be deserves to be told. Participating in a congregation also offers its people a means for relating to what they regard as sacred and true.

This is the story of the liberal religious tradition and how it has been expressed in one specific region: Washington, D.C. Religious liberalism is not the possession of any one organization; its values find expression in many faith communities. But the primary associations of congregations espousing religious liberalism in the United States have been the American Unitarian Association and the Universalist Church of America. In 1961, these two organizations merged to create the Unitarian Universalist Association.

The roots of Unitarianism reach back to the early Christian church and its debates about the nature of Jesus. Some regarded Jesus as a man with a special relationship to God and a divine mission that came from that relationship, but they did not believe Jesus was God. This interpretation contrasted with the doctrine of the Trinity, which states that the Father, Jesus Christ, and the Holy Spirit are equal expressions of God. Those who believed that God was supreme and that Jesus was not equal to God became known as Unitarians.

In American churches, Unitarianism was less a statement about the nature of Jesus than it was a cluster of theological ideas that gradually developed in congregations of the Puritan tradition, primarily in New England. The decades prior to and following the American Revolution were a time of theological ferment, as churches adapted to the reality of a new nation, with a life experience different from what had been left behind. Early American Unitarians—who preferred to be known as liberal Christians, practical Christians, or just Christians—rejected the traditional Puritan belief in the essential sinfulness of humanity in favor of a more optimistic view of human possibility. They regarded the capacities of reason and reflection on human experience as valid methods for evaluating religious truth. They also rejected creedal statements as inadequate attempts to define and control the holy. Instead, they promoted freedom as offering a more authentic pathway to determining religious truth.

Universalism is defined as a belief in universal salvation: that all people will be saved, that none will be consigned by a loving God to eternal punishment. As with Unitarianism, Universalism dates back to the early years of the Christian church. The Universalists believed that a God of love would not divide the world into those who were saved and those who were damned. They declared that God would not give up on any of His people, always offering the possibility of salvation.

Universalism in America dates to 1770 when an English Universalist named John Murray began preaching his message of universal salvation throughout New England and along America's East Coast. Others took up this banner, and Universalist churches were established with their distinctive message of "No hell!" Theirs was a God of love who could be trusted to guide each person along his or her own path to salvation.

American Unitarianism and Universalism also developed within the context of a set of ideas whose influence was pervasive during the early years of this new nation. The philosophy of the Enlightenment emphasized free inquiry, human experience, and rationality over religious and social dogma. It opposed tyranny in all its forms and promoted freedom and reason as the most trustworthy foundations for a government and a society. The values of the Enlightenment were incorporated in many of the founding documents of the American nation, including the Declaration of Independence and the Bill of Rights.

American Unitarians sought to apply the same values of freedom and reason to religion. For them, the political and religious realms were related. A democratic government gave citizens the power to evaluate its policies and participate in changing them when deemed necessary. For the Unitarians, that same process of rational evaluation in a context of freedom offered the best opportunity for an authentic religious faith.

American Universalists offered a less intellectual approach, focusing on what it meant to live in relationship to a God whose essential nature is love. But the practice of that faith brought them to many positions similar to that of the Unitarians. Universalism was also a non-creedal religion that offered its members the freedom to determine their own beliefs. And as with the Unitarians, they affirmed a God more concerned with promoting what is best in humanity than in punishing what is worst.

A story of congregations throughout years and generations is a story of change anchored by core values. It is the story of how people in different eras have sought to apply the affirmations of their tradition to the always-changing realities of life in this world. So too it is with the Unitarians and Universalists of Washington, D.C. The changes from the beginnings to the present are substantial. Yet the central values remain: freedom and reason in religion, an emphasis on human worth and dignity, a God or force of life that can be trusted to lead people to what is right and true.

Churches are human institutions. As such, their actions are sometimes admirable, sometimes not. The stands they take are sometimes forward thinking, but at other times, they represent retreat and retrenchment. Anyone who looks to a church as a consistent beacon of righteousness is likely to be disappointed. Congregational life can be messy.

Perhaps a better approach is to view congregations as laboratories: contexts in which those who seek to be faithful to a set of values and ideals work out what that might mean in today's world. In church, people may debate what they are called to do and be, argue specifics of how they are to be people of faith, undertake projects that sometimes work and sometimes don't. At their best, churches promote a dynamic engagement with their tradition, offering opportunities to express its vision in everyday life.

This is a story told through photographs. My hope is that readers might get a sense for the real people who have been Unitarians and Universalists in the past and who are Unitarian Universalists today. Looking back through the generations with changing styles of clothes and dress, different methods of expression, even different vocabularies, it is still possible to find points of connection. There is a continuity in what these congregations have been and what they are. Despite the differences, we are kin.

One

BEGINNINGS IN WASHINGTON

In 1820, Washington, D.C., was more idea than reality. Founded 30 years before as the nation's new capital, it was slow to develop. Washington, D.C., was described as a city of streets without houses, devoid of a community water supply or sewage system, where farm animals roamed without restraint, and with dirt streets that kicked up endless dust in the summer and mired traffic in mud when it rained.

On the evening of July 31, 1820, a small group of men gathered in a room above the public baths on C Street. Their intent was to establish a new church in Washington. Thomas Bulfinch, a Bostonian who had come to Washington to start a business, was appointed secretary. He recorded the results, which read, in part, "Resolved: that it is expedient that measures be taken for erecting a place of divine worship upon Unitarian principles in the City of Washington." The beginnings of an institutional Unitarian presence in the Washington area date to that meeting.

Universalists were slower to organize in Washington, yet they were also represented. In 1827, an itinerate Universalist preacher named Theophilus Fiske presented a sermon in Washington's city hall. It is the first known Universalist service in the capital city. In subsequent years, Universalist ministers occasionally came through the city, but efforts to organize a congregation were not successful until after the Civil War.

Unitarians enjoyed prominence in the early days of Washington, attracting many who held positions of power in local and national government. Among the founding members of First Unitarian Church of Washington were a future U.S. president, a future U.S. vice president, two who would serve as mayor of the city, and a nationally known architect. Unitarians were well represented among the leaders who shaped the fortunes of this new nation.

The United States had been founded on principles of freedom and reason in government. The First Unitarian Church of Washington offered a religious community guided by these same ideals. The church attracted those who questioned dogma and who believed in the human capacity for creating a society that best met the needs of its people.

At a meeting of the friends of Unitarian Christianity held at the Society's room in C street, on the evening of Monday the 31st ult. Moses Young being called to the ... and Thomas Bulfinch appointed secretary, on mot ... William Elliot, it was

Resolved That it is expedient that measures be taken for erecting a place of divine worship upon Unitarian principles, in the City of Washington.

Resolved That an adjourned meeting of the friends of Unitarian Christianity be held at this place on Sunday the 6th inst at 5 o'clock, P.M. for the purpose of concerting measures to effect the object of the foregoing resolution.

by order of the chairman

Thomas Bulfinch sec'y.

August 1st 1820.

Unitarian worship in the Washington area began as early as 1815, when a group of English Unitarians met in members' homes in Georgetown. But a congregation was not organized until 1821, when the First Unitarian Church of Washington was established. This photograph is of minutes from a meeting held on July 31, 1820, which signaled the intent of participants to create such a church. (ASC.)

Robert Little was an English Unitarian minister who had left his native land and the restrictions imposed upon those not participating in the Church of England. He came to Washington in 1819 intending to establish himself in a business but was called into service by Unitarians in the community. When First Unitarian Church was organized, the congregation elected Little its first minister. (ASC.)

Little established himself as a brave and eloquent speaker who argued for the right of each individual "to judge for himself" on matters of faith. He applied the test of reason to religious claims and sought to find rational explanations for the "miracles" of the Bible. When he died unexpectedly in 1827, he was mourned by Unitarians and non-Unitarians alike. (ASC.)

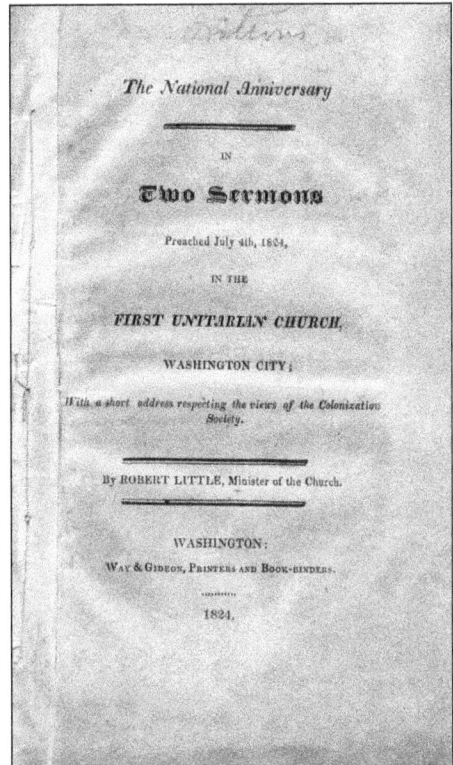

The National Anniversary

IN

Two Sermons

Preached July 4th, 1824,

IN THE

FIRST UNITARIAN CHURCH,

WASHINGTON CITY;

With a short address respecting the views of the Colonization Society.

By ROBERT LITTLE, Minister of the Church.

WASHINGTON:
WAY & GIDEON, PRINTERS AND BOOK-BINDERS.

1824.

Unitarians were well represented among statesmen during Washington's early years. Edward Everett, a Unitarian minister, was a congressman and senator from Massachusetts. He was appointed Secretary of State by Pres. Millard Fillmore (a Unitarian) upon the death of Daniel Webster (also a Unitarian). His nephew Edward Everett Hale served briefly as minister of Washington's First Unitarian Church. (ASC.)

Originally a lay Methodist preacher in England, John Murray became convinced of the Universalist message of a loving God who would not create hell as a place of eternal punishment. Murray's subsequent excommunication from the Methodist Church and several personal tragedies—including the deaths of his wife and son—brought him to become disillusioned with organized religion, and he came to America for a fresh start. (UUA.)

Murray had vowed never to preach again, but fate intervened when his ship from England ran aground off New Jersey's coast. On shore, he met a farmer named Thomas Potter who had built a meetinghouse, waiting for a preacher with a message that spoke to his heart. Potter convinced Murray to preach, and Murray's sermon on universal grace was what Potter had been waiting for. (UUA.)

FIRST CHURCH IN GLOUCESTER

Encouraged by the response of Potter and his neighbors, Murray rediscovered his call to the ministry and preached his message of "No hell!" to audiences throughout the northeast. He settled in Gloucester, Massachusetts, where a congregation gathered around him. They built a simple church and on Christmas Day 1780 held their first service. This was the first Universalist church built in America. (UUA.)

Theophilus Fiske was a Universalist minister of uneven reputation, described as "brainy but unreliable." Nevertheless he found a way to deliver a sermon at the city hall in Washington on December 16, 1827; it was the first Universalist sermon preached in Washington. In this "discourse," Fiske testified for universal salvation, "when all shall know the Lord from the least to the greatest." (AHTL.)

A DISCOURSE

DELIVERED AT

THE CITY HALL, WASHINGTON, D. C.,

ON

Sunday Afternoon, Dec. 16, 1827,

AND REPEATED

AT TROY, N. Y.

On the first Sunday in August, 1828.

BY T. FISK,

Pastor of the Lombard Street Church, Philadelphia.

PHILADELPHIA:
Printed by John Young, 3. Black Horse Alley, South Second Street.

13

John Quincy Adams was a founding member of First Unitarian Church of Washington. He was a loyal church member who continued his support when he became president of the United States and then a congressman from Massachusetts. Ministers noted that he was a demanding parishioner, impatient with careless reasoning. (UUA.)

A Southerner, John C. Calhoun encountered Unitarianism while a student at Yale. He became a leading figure in Washington as representative from South Carolina, Secretary of War, and then U.S. vice president under his political rival Adams. Calhoun was a proponent of states' rights and a defender of slavery, and he and Adams were often in opposition. Yet they both helped found First Unitarian Church. (UUA.)

Among early tasks undertaken by the founders was to solicit funds to build, "a church for the use of a society of Unitarians." This ledger shows pledges from Adams and Calhoun (left column, about two-thirds down), as well as the notation that they paid in full. (ASC.)

The architect Charles Bulfinch moved to Washington in 1818 to complete construction of the U.S. Capitol, which had been damaged in the War of 1812. In Boston, the Bulfinch family was Unitarian, and so they were attracted to the project of creating a liberal church in Washington. Bulfinch designed the congregation's first church building. (UUA.)

Contemporary accounts called Charles Bulfinch's design for First Unitarian Church of Washington "simple but elegant" and an important addition to the developing city. Located at the corner of Sixth and D Streets, just north of Pennsylvania Avenue, it was in close proximity to government offices and residences of those in power. Daniel Webster, who served as representative, senator, and Secretary of State, lived next door and attended First Unitarian Church—according to a quip of the time—when he was not worshipping the Constitution or himself. The building was dedicated in 1822 with more than 400 people attending. Robert Little, in his dedication sermon, anticipated that, "These walls will, I trust, bear witness that our lives have not been altogether useless to mankind. Some I hope may be better for our exertions in the cause of truth." This building served the congregation until 1877. (ASC.)

Bulfinch contacted Joseph Revere, son of Paul Revere, to cast a bell for the new church's tower. In this reply, Joseph proposes a bell that he would guarantee for one year. A serious fire had made it evident that a warning bell was needed to alert the population to dangers, and Pres. James Monroe contributed money to help purchase it. (ASC.)

The Revere Bell warned Washington of dangers from 1822 until 1859, when the church authorized that the bell toll after the execution of John Brown, the abolitionist. Members of Congress, angry at the political use of the bell, removed it from its public role. But this bell that was guaranteed to last one year continues to ring—now in its third building—for human rights causes. (ASC.)

17

Robert Little died in 1827 on a family vacation in Pennsylvania after having preached what one listener reported as "one of the greatest sermons I ever heard." Even those who disagreed with him theologically testified to his sincerity, integrity, and personal warmth. Frederick Farley, pictured here, officiated at the memorial service and later served briefly as minister of the Washington church. (ASC.)

Washington Unitarians had a hard time keeping their ministers. Between 1827 and the start of the Civil War in 1861, twelve ministers served the congregation, some for less than a year. Casneau Palfrey, Harvard educated and well regarded for his literary abilities, stayed for six years, but the church did not prosper during his tenure. (ASC.)

Stephen Bulfinch, son of architect Charles Bulfinch, was called to the Washington pulpit in 1830 and became the congregation's fourth minister. While serving the Washington church, he invited Lucretia Mott, the Quaker feminist and reformer, to speak from the pulpit of his congregation, a daring move for the times. (ASC.)

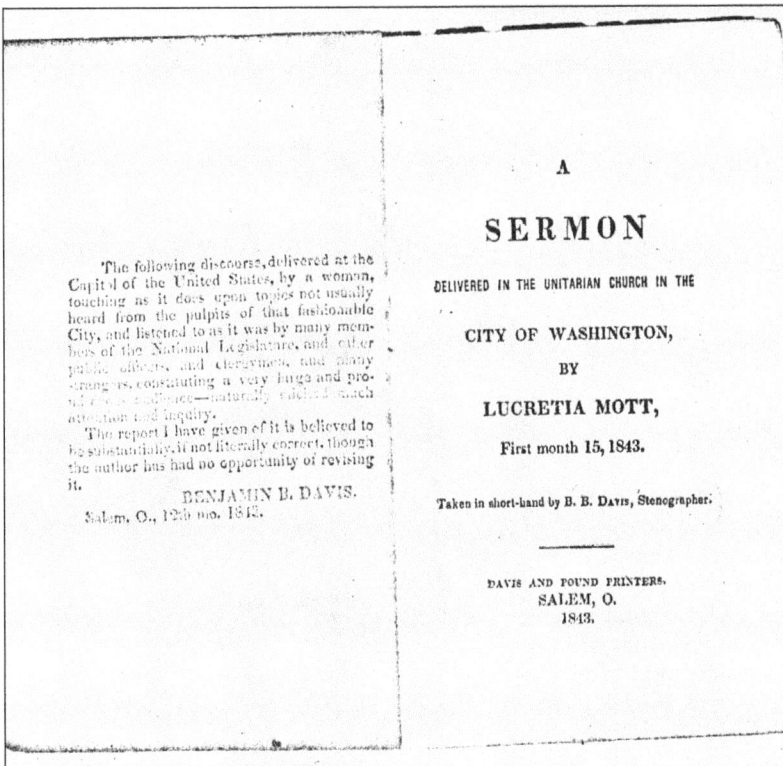

A

SERMON

DELIVERED IN THE UNITARIAN CHURCH IN THE

CITY OF WASHINGTON,

BY

LUCRETIA MOTT,

First month 15, 1843.

Taken in short-hand by B. B. Davis, Stenographer.

———

DAVIS AND POUND PRINTERS,
SALEM, O.
1843.

The following discourse, delivered at the Capitol of the United States, by a woman, touching as it does upon topics not usually heard from the pulpits of that fashionable City, and listened to as it was by many members of the National Legislature, and other public officers, and clergymen, and many strangers, constituting a very large and promiscuous audience—naturally excited much attention and inquiry.

The report I have given of it is believed to be substantially, if not literally correct, though the author has had no opportunity of revising it.

BENJAMIN B. DAVIS.
Salem, O., 12th mo. 1843.

The presentation of a sermon by Mott at First Unitarian Church created a stir. Not only was it unusual for a woman to occupy the pulpit, but the causes she advanced were not of the mainstream: women's rights, abolition of slavery, peace, and temperance. A congregation of many national and community leaders crowded into the church to hear her. (ASC.)

Slavery divided Washingtonians, as it did Americans. The city had been largely built by slaves, and it had a large slave population. Unitarians in Washington were also divided. Samuel Longfellow, brother of Henry Wadsworth Longfellow, served the Washington church briefly in 1847. In a sermon he called slavery "a great evil," but the congregation's response convinced him that they would not accept an abolitionist as minister. (ASC.)

Despite its divisions, the congregation called an outspoken abolitionist to be its minister in 1854. Moncure Conway was a Southerner from a Methodist slave-owning family who became a Unitarian. His passionate opposition to slavery distressed the more sedate congregation, and after a particularly strong sermon—he recalled that after the sermon "the choir did not sing"—the church dismissed him. (ASC.)

In 1850, Congress passed the Fugitive Slave Act, requiring that escaped slaves in the free states be returned to their owners. The law was hated in the North, and while some Unitarians fought against it, others played key roles in its passage. Daniel Webster, a Unitarian, promoted it as a compromise to save the Union. Pres. Millard Fillmore, shown here, was also a Unitarian. He signed the bill into law. (UUA.)

William Henry Channing, nephew of William Ellery Channing, was a transcendentalist poet and social activist who fiercely opposed slavery. He became minister of First Unitarian Church in 1861 and guided the congregation through the Civil War years, offering the church as a hospital. In return, the congregation used the Senate Chamber for Sunday worship. (*Unitarian Universalist Association. Inactive Minister Files, 1825–1999. bMS 1446. AHTL.*)

21

Universalist Church,
Church of Our Father
Washington, D. C.

Unitarians and Universalists encountered challenges as the nation emerged from the Civil War. First Unitarian Church faced a dwindling congregation, substantial debt, and an uncertainty of purpose that led the congregation to consider affiliating with another denomination. Universalists had still not established a church in the nation's capital, despite several efforts by visiting ministers. Yet, by the 1870s, the fortunes of both Unitarians and Universalists in Washington were changing. Unitarians built a new church to replace the old and decaying Bulfinch building. Universalists organized their first Washington congregation and then, in 1883, moved into their first building (pictured here), located on Thirteenth and L Streets, northwest, just a block away from the Unitarian church. As the 20th century approached, both Unitarians and Universalists experienced a renewal of energy and purpose. (Church of Our Father, Washington, D.C., *Unitarian Universalist Association*, bms00349, Andover-Harvard Theological Library, Harvard Divinity School, Harvard University.)

Two

CHALLENGING TIMES

The years following the Civil War were difficult for Unitarians and Universalists in Washington. Unitarians boasted prominent members and visitors—Pres. Abraham Lincoln attended First Unitarian Church on at least one occasion, and the African American leader Frederick Douglass frequently participated. But the church itself struggled to be a viable institution. Ministers rarely stayed more than a few years. The finances were precarious. And the Charles Bulfinch–designed church building fell into disrepair.

The Universalists had not yet established a church in the nation's capital. At the time, Universalism was growing dramatically in the Northeast and the Midwest, but Washington was beyond its sphere of influence. At the Universalist General Convention of 1868, a proposal was made that a national church be established in the nation's capital. It would not just be a local congregation but also a cathedral church for all Universalists. The proposal was tabled and revisited occasionally for the next 56 years.

Despite these challenges, the fortunes of both Unitarianism and Universalism in Washington improved as the 20th century approached. With help from the national Unitarian organization, the Washington congregation firmed up its membership, built a new church, and reorganized under a new name, All Souls Church.

Universalists in Washington finally succeeded in establishing a congregation, though it was less than the national church envisioned in 1868. The new congregation met in rented quarters until 1883, when they moved into their new church. Washington's Unitarian and Universalist churches were located just a block from each other, but their contacts were infrequent. The two congregations lived in largely separate worlds.

Despite the challenges, there were successes in extending the reach of religious liberalism. The Universalist Clara Barton established the American Red Cross, anticipating the involvement of religious organizations in providing care for those afflicted by natural disasters and outbreaks of illness. And both Unitarians and Universalists established outreach efforts in Japan, anticipating international involvement in both groups. It was a time when both Unitarians and Universalists considered their roles in the larger society and the contributions they might make.

Clara Barton grew up in a Universalist family. When an accident rendered her brother an invalid, she attended to him, gaining experience in giving care. As an adult, she became a teacher, then a clerk in the Patent Office in Washington, D.C. During the Civil War, she volunteered on the battlefield, where she brought supplies for soldiers and nursed the wounded and sick. (UNMC.)

When the Franco-Prussian War broke out in Europe, Barton volunteered her services to the recently established International Red Cross. Upon returning to the United States, she founded the American Red Cross and personally supervised humanitarian aid to those affected by emergencies such as floods, epidemics, and hurricanes. The photograph is of the first Red Cross headquarters, located on Vermont Avenue NW. (UNMC.)

The end of the Civil War left the nation depleted and in need of restoration; so too was the status of the First Unitarian Church. William Henry Channing resigned his ministry, and the church found itself with a reduced membership and in substantial debt. Furthermore, the Bulfinch building had become sadly dilapidated. Enthusiasm for Unitarianism waned, and a movement began to reorganize First Unitarian Church as a Congregational church. (ASC.)

Frederick Allen Hinckley was installed as minister in 1870. He initiated educational programs and social groups, and also sought assistance from Unitarians nationwide to build a more suitable church. A barrier to growth was removed when uncertainty about Washington's continued status as the U.S. capital ended. Some had wanted the seat of government to be more centrally located in the nation. (ASC.)

The year 1877 was significant for Washington Unitarians. Clay MacCauley was called as minister, fresh from two years of advanced study in Germany. In the same year, the National Unitarian Conference voted funding to help build a new church in Washington. And First Unitarian Church reorganized as All Souls Church. It was a new beginning. (ASC.)

The congregation's new name removed "Unitarian" from its title—or consigned it to the end, as in "All Souls Church, Unitarian." The reasoning that drove this change is not entirely clear, but it was likely an effort to be more inclusive. Universalists in Washington, for example, often attended this church since there was not yet a local Universalist congregation. The new name welcomed a larger constituency. (ASC.)

The photograph is of the new All Souls Church at Fourteenth and L Streets. Its mission was articulated by MacCauley, who said, "It is of importance to the general interests of rational Christianity that at the seat of the National Government there should be a place where Unitarians from different sections of the country may meet." Unitarians in the late 19th century viewed themselves as promoting a reasoned and reasonable Christianity. In an age of skepticism about religious claims, Unitarians offered a faith that removed elements difficult to reconcile to the modern mind. Their message was that one could be both religious and rational. (ASC.)

At first glance, the sanctuary at the new All Souls Church looks like many Protestant churches of the era, with its cavernous worship space, dark wood, Gothic design touches, and the Lord's Prayer featured on the right-front wall. Unitarians struggled with competing impulses—on one hand to be accepted within the larger community of Christian churches, on the other hand to maintain the distinctiveness of its history and message. The church sought to clarify what it stood for with a statement on the front of each Sunday bulletin. "This Church is dedicated to religion, but not to a creed . . . Love to God and man and the perfecting of our spiritual nature it regards as the unchanging substance of religion and the essential gospel of Jesus . . . It welcomes to its worship and fellowship all who are in sympathy with a religion thus simple and thus free." (ASC.)

Order of Exercises

AT THE

DEDICATION

OF

All Souls' Church,

WASHINGTON, D. C.

AND AT THE

INSTALLATION

OF

REV. CLAY MacCAULEY

AS PASTOR,

ON

Tuesday and Wednesday Evenings, January 29, 30, 1878.

SERMONS

BY

HENRY W. BELLOWS, D. D., OF NEW YORK,

AND

JOHN F. W. WARE, OF BOSTON, MASS.

1821 1877

ALL SOULS CHURCH

GIBSON BROTHERS, PRINTERS

The new All Souls Church was dedicated on January 29, 1878, with Ambrose Burnside, a Union general in the Civil War, presiding. Those attending included Hannibal Hamlin, who had been U.S. vice president during Abraham Lincoln's first term, and William Greenleaf Eliot, founder of Washington University in St. Louis. (ASC.)

The stained-glass windows in the new All Souls Church sanctuary reveal a more traditional Christian orientation than would develop in later years. On the left, Jesus comforts one who suffers. On the right, he offers his teachings to children. It was a gentle Christianity that focused on service to humanity as the highest form of religion. (ASC.)

The tenure of Clay MacCauley as minister of All Souls Church was to last only until 1880. He resigned the position and went on to other pursuits, including work with Native American communities. He then went to Japan, where he served for almost 25 years as director of a Unitarian mission in that nation. (UUA.)

The Clay MacCauley Memorial *Tōrō*, Mita, Tokyo, Japan.

Unlike other Christian missionary efforts in Japan, the Unitarian mission was not concerned with establishing churches. Instead, it sought to promote understanding among religions and brought people together in affirmation of universal truths. MacCauley was decorated by the Japanese emperor with "The Order of the Rising Sun" in 1909, and this memorial was erected in Tokyo. (UUA.)

Mr Joseph Stewart — 2d Asst P.M.G. P.O.D.

To All Souls' Church, Dr.

For Rent of 2 Seats in Pew No. 53 for the quarter ending September 30th, 1910, $ 10

" " November 31st 1910 $ 20

Received Payment December 12 19__

Chas E Hood, Treasurer

CHAS. E. HOOD
TREASURER
PACIFIC BUILDING

Pew Rents are made payable in advance. Pew-holders wishing to give up their pews will please notify the Treasurer at least fifteen days before the close of the quarter. The Treasurer will appreciate remittance by check, mailed to his office. They may also be made by means of sealed envelope—addressed to him—and placed in collection baskets at church.

Washington, D. C., April 1, 1910

To All Souls' Church, Dr.

For Rent of 2 Seats in Pew No. 53 for the quarter ending June 30th, 1910, $

Received Payment April 6th 1910

Chas E Hood, Treasurer

CHAS. E. HOOD
TREASURER
PACIFIC BUILDING

Pew Rents are made payable in advance. Pew-holders wishing to give up their pews will please notify the Treasurer at least fifteen days before the close of the quarter. The Treasurer will appreciate remittance by check, mailed to his office. They may also be made by means of sealed envelope—addressed to him—and placed in collection baskets at church.

Paying to rent a pew in church was a method of financing common to Protestant and Catholic churches. However, it suggested an exclusivity that was reinforced by the announcement in the weekly bulletin, "Applications for pews or sittings should be made to Mr. Hood at the close of any service." Pew rentals were later discontinued as All Souls Church sought to actually welcome all souls. (ASC.)

The ministry of Rush Rees Shippen initiated a period of sustained growth. An experienced parish minister, he also served as secretary of the American Unitarian Association before coming to Washington. Shippen was active in social outreach, serving on the board of Howard University and helping Clara Barton create the American Red Cross. (ASC.)

After decades of unsuccessful efforts in Washington, Universalists moved into their new church building in 1883. In the dedication service, Rev. A. B. Grosh offered the hope that, "by our enlightenment others may be enlightened, and be sent forth fully equipped for the battle of life." First Universalist Church later became known as Church of Our Father. (*Unitarian Universalist Association archives*, bms00902, AHTL.)

Sermon and Addresses at the Opening of the

FIRST UNIVERSALIST CHURCH,

COR. 13TH AND L STREETS, WASHINGTON, D. C.

Edward Everett Hale (left) was a Unitarian minister and author of *The Man Without A Country*. He served briefly as minister of Washington's Unitarian church in the pre–Civil War years and later returned to serve as chaplain to the U.S. Senate. In this photograph, he is shown with Ulysses G. B. Pierce, who was called to All Souls Church in 1901. (ASC.)

A new church building calls for heavy machinery. Here the minister of All Souls Church, Ulysses G. B. Pierce (standing in the cab of the steam shovel), joins other church officials for the ceremonial first shovelful of earth to begin construction on the Harvard Street facilities. The congregation had outgrown its 1877 building, and by the early 1900s, there was call for a new church. The desire for a new building was not just to gain more space; it was also to make a statement about the growing influence of Unitarians in Washington. The desire was for a building that expressed the simple and open theology of Unitarianism and facilities that made possible more involvement in the surrounding community. (ASC.)

Three

Unitarians in the 20th Century

The year 1901 saw the beginning of what was to become the longest ministry at All Souls Church. Ulysses G. B. Pierce began a tenure that would last until his death in 1943 and that would usher in a period of growth and prosperity whose high point was the erection of a new church building on Harvard Street in northwest Washington. That building remains in use today.

Previous to calling Pierce, the congregation had entertained the prospect of making what would have been—for the times—a dramatic statement. With the pulpit open in 1900, there was substantial sentiment to call a woman as minister. Ida C. Hultin, whose ordination was recognized by both the Unitarians and the Universalists, had recently addressed the Women's Suffrage Convention. She was a powerful speaker who deeply impressed those who met her. But the possibility of her becoming minister of All Souls Church set off a controversy that was decided when the congregation voted not to pursue this possibility.

The 20th century brought new visibility for Unitarianism in Washington, as the nation elected a Unitarian as president. William Howard Taft was a committed Unitarian in his hometown of Cincinnati. When he came to Washington in 1908 to assume the duties of the presidency, he joined All Souls Church and became an active participant in the congregation.

Taft's presidency was not successful, as he found himself locked in struggles with Congress and was unable to establish his own agenda. He turned to his faith and All Souls Church as a source of comfort and renewal. After being defeated in his bid for reelection, Taft expressed gratitude for the church that had sustained him through difficult times. Later he was to return to Washington in a new role: chief justice of the Supreme Court. He then resumed participation in All Souls Church as the church's best-known member.

As president of the United States, William Howard Taft (shown here, second from the left) regularly attended services at All Souls Church. During the campaign, he had been attacked by agents of his opponent, William Jennings Bryan, because his church did not have a creed expressing belief in the divinity of Jesus Christ. Pres. Theodore Roosevelt, who had picked Taft to succeed him, sprang to his defense, attending First Unitarian Church with the nominee. Ulysses G. B. Pierce, minister of All Souls Church, defended Taft and Unitarianism, stating that Unitarians follow the religion of Jesus, not the religion about Jesus. Here Taft is pictured with other prominent laymen at the beginning of a major fund-raising effort in support of the American Unitarian Association. This photograph features (from left to right) Harvard University president Charles Eliot, Taft, Richard M. Saltonstall, and Ernest G. Adams (ASC.)

The Meaning of Christmas

AS EXPLAINED TO THE

Sunday School Children of All Souls' Unitarian Church

WASHINGTON, D. C.

BY

William Howard Taft

President of the United States

DECEMBER 24, 1911

I ONLY come to share Christmas Greetings with you, and not to give them to you, for I am not used to speaking to Sunday Schools, and I do not know that I can talk the language to which you are accustomed. The only thing I want to say is that Christmas is a development, and that you will realize it as you grow older. The first thing about Christmas is the pleasure you have in receiving gifts, the pleasure you have in the fact that somebody thinks enough of you to give you something. For a time you will think a good deal of the value of the gift, and after that of the good will toward you that prompts the gift. Then after a time, as I hope, when you are all able to make gifts, you will begin to think of the pleasure you have in making the gifts, rather than of the pleasure you have in receiving them. In other words, the growth of Christmas will be the growth of the idea that it is more blessed to give than to receive. You will find it right in your own life. The lasting joy that you have in serving somebody else and in doing something for somebody will ultimately impress itself on you, so that Christmas will mean a great deal more to you in the future than it means now — much as it now means to you. I wish you a Merry Christmas, and hope that you will all remember what I have told you. If it does not prove to be true, come and tell me about it, and I will prove it to you.

On Christmas Eve, 1911, President Taft spoke to the children in the Sunday school of All Schools Church. He described Christmas as a time when humanity is reminded of the value of giving to others. He did not refer to the story of the birth of Jesus. For most Unitarians of the time, the Biblical account of the first Christmas did not survive the test of reason and was not considered historical fact. Instead, they sought more universal meanings to Christmas, such as, "it is more blessed to give than to receive," or that "it is in service to others that we find our own deepest satisfaction." President Taft's approach to Christmas is reminiscent of an earlier Unitarian, Charles Dickens, for whom the hope of Christmas was that it might awaken the spirit of generosity and compassion. (ASC.)

By 1901, the leadership at All Souls Church was expressing the desire for a new church building. The congregation had grown, as had the religious education program for children, and the church had assumed a new prominence in the community. In 1913, the church had purchased property on Sixteenth Street near R Street in northwest Washington, and plans were sufficiently advanced to hold a cornerstone-laying ceremony in which Pres. William Howard Taft agreed to participate. President Taft, shown seated to the left of the speaker, was soon to complete his term as president. Dressed on this February day in a fur-lined coat and bustling with characteristic good humor, he dominated the spectacle. The speaker in this photograph is Samuel A. Eliot, president of the American Unitarian Association. (ASC.)

In this photograph, President Taft lays the cornerstone for the new church. When leaving the presidency, President Taft offered a farewell to the All Souls Church congregation. "My father was a Unitarian; my mother was a Unitarian; my grandmother was a Unitarian, and it has always been a wonder to me that all the world has not become Unitarian. But I think it is verging in that direction." (ASC.)

Its planners envisioned a cathedral-like structure, but even though the cornerstone had been laid, the rest of the building was not to be. The project was abandoned, and preparations commenced for a different building on a different site. Meanwhile, President Taft's "farewell" turned out to be premature. In 1921, he returned to Washington, having been appointed chief justice of the Supreme Court. (ASC.)

In 1901, Ulysses G. B. Pierce was called to be minister of All Souls Church. He had studied for the ministry as a Baptist but was dissatisfied with orthodoxy and became a Unitarian. He and his wife, Florence L. Pierce, who was also ordained, helped transform All Souls Church from a struggling institution into one of the strongest Unitarian churches in the nation. (ASC.)

‹‹‹‹‹‹‹‹‹‹‹‹‹‹‹‹‹‹‹‹‹‹‹‹‹‹‹‹‹‹‹‹‹‹‹‹‹

A Reasonable Easter

By ULYSSES G. B. PIERCE, D.D.

Author, preacher, and missionary. Minister of All Souls'
Church, Washington, D. C.

〜

[No. 196]

PUBLISHED FOR FREE DISTRIBUTION
AMERICAN UNITARIAN ASSOCIATION
25 BEACON STREET, BOSTON, MASS.

‹‹‹‹‹‹‹‹‹‹‹‹‹‹‹‹‹‹‹‹‹‹‹‹‹‹‹‹‹‹‹‹‹‹‹‹‹

If Christmas could be made reasonable, why not Easter? In this sermon, Reverend Pierce responded to the challenge by asserting that belief in an afterlife is completely rational, embedded in human beings as a foretaste of a glorious future. "That there is . . . awaiting us something better than dust and ashes ought not seriously to be questioned," he said. (ASC.)

After the demise of the previous building project, planners found a new site for a church at the corner of Sixteenth and Harvard Streets in northwest Washington. The property was owned by the widow of a senator from Colorado. She agreed to sell it to the church because she wished to maintain the architectural quality on what was then called Upper Sixteenth Street. (ASC.)

Funding for the new building came both from the congregation and from the American Unitarian Association. An architectural competition was held to solicit designs for the building. Guidelines included a structure that "should typify Unitarian ideals and harmony" as well as "harmonize with the architecture of Washington." This cornerstone ceremony took place on November 7, 1922. (ASC.)

The winning design was modeled after a historic church in London, St. Martin-in-the-Fields, located in Trafalgar Square and pictured here. The Georgian Colonial style was characteristic of New England Unitarian churches. The principle architect was Henry R. Shepley, who also designed several buildings at Harvard University. (ASC.)

In this photograph, building stones for the new church lay waiting on the construction site. Throughout the early 20th century, there was a strong Unitarian presence in Washington. Indicative of that influence, two Unitarian ministers were appointed chaplain of the U.S. Senate: Edward Everett Hale and Ulysses G. B. Pierce. (ASC.)

Pictured here is work on the foundation of the Harvard Street church. The American nation was emerging from World War I. Construction of this new building expressed the optimism with which the country entered the postwar period. (ASC.)

The congregation vacated the previous building two years before the new building was to become available. During the hiatus between buildings, the church met for services at the Knickerbocher Theater. Attendance on the first Sunday after leaving the old church was greater than the capacity its sanctuary had been. Here the steeple on the new church goes up. (ASC.)

A newspaper account noted the "unique activities" held at this new facility. There were "moving pictures on Sunday nights and foreign language talking films Saturday night." An amateur theater group presented plays, and community groups used the fellowship hall regularly. There was a recreation room, including a basketball court and shower rooms. The Police Boys' Club used the facility, and later, during World War II, the church became Saturday night sleeping quarters for servicemen visiting Washington. The young people's club sponsored dances, the Women's Alliance featured speakers from the community, a "Current Problems" class sponsored discussions of foreign policy issues, and a course on "Great Liberals" offered an opportunity to delve into the writings of, well, great liberals. The dream that involved the church becoming more active in the life of the Washington community was taking shape. (ASC.)

The contrast with the previous sanctuary was dramatic. The dark and heavy L Street church was replaced with a space characterized by openness and light—yet it had a more intimate feeling. The lack of specific religious symbolism in the new sanctuary was a faithful reflection of the style of early New England Unitarian churches. It was to be a church for all souls. (ASC.)

These new pews were not for rent, as the pew rental system was abandoned. Despite the church's advocacy of a democratic faith, congregational votes had been weighted to favor those who paid for the most "sittings." The effect of this change was to double the number of people voting in congregational meetings and increased participation throughout the church. (ASC.)

The dedication for the new All Souls Church was held on Sunday, October 26, 1924, with both morning and evening services. Pres. Calvin Coolidge and his wife, Grace Coolidge, attended, as did dignitaries from the Washington community and the larger Unitarian world. (ASC.)

Supreme Court of the United States.
Washington, D.C.

October 25, 1924.

My dear Mr. Ricker:

I have your kind invitation to attend the reception at All Souls' Church on Monday evening, October 27th. Mrs. Taft and I expect to be present, but as I don't go out in the evening, and find it unwise to stand up in line and receive, you will have to excuse me, because I shall have to slip out and go home immediately after the exercises.

Sincerely yours,

Wm H Taft

Mr. George A. Ricker,
Chairman, Reception Committee,
All Souls Church,
Washington, D. C.

William Howard Taft's primary ambition had been to serve as chief justice of the Supreme Court. That was finally realized in 1921, when Pres. Warren G. Harding appointed him to the post. He returned to Washington and resumed his participation at All Souls Church. (ASC.)

The new All Souls Church was conceived as both a local parish and a national church. The *Christian Register*, a Unitarian publication, said, "Every Unitarian who goes to Washington and visits the Church of his faith there is assured of a thrill that he has not experienced in his lifetime." Pictured here are representatives to the Unitarian General Conference in 1925. (ASC.)

Religious education had been slow to develop an approach distinct to religious liberalism, and classes for children throughout the 19th century used the same materials as trinitarian Protestant churches. That began to change in the early 20th century when programs for children de-emphasized rote memorization of Bible passages and focused instead on building character. (ASC.)

Unitarians in Washington devoted more resources to children's programming than was customary, and the All Souls Sunday school became the largest in the country among Unitarian churches. Yet space was still inadequate for demand, and classes crowded into the dining room with curtain dividers creating individual rooms. Pictured here are children at a May Queen Festival. (ASC.)

The largest organization at All Souls Church was the Women's Alliance, which had been organized in 1896. Alliance activities included a catering committee that provided food service to outside organizations. At the time, the All Souls dining room was one of the few places in Washington that served integrated groups, bringing Eleanor Roosevelt to visit on several occasions. This photograph dates from 1931. (ASC.)

The owner of a fashionable department store in Washington, Julius Garfinkel, provided funds in his will for "needy and worthy" members of All Souls Church. Thus, Unitarian House for Ladies came into being, providing living space for elderly women of the church. The house was purchased with funds from the bequest and furnished by members of the congregation. (ASC.)

This facility, located at 1802 Park Road NW, functioned for 14 years. When the city revised requirements for nursing homes in Washington, the cost of compliance went beyond what the congregation could afford, and Unitarian House for Ladies was closed. These residents relax under the watchful eye of their minister, Ulysses G. B. Pierce, whose portrait looks down from the wall. (ASC.)

The Universalist General Convention, an assembly of Universalists from across the nation, met in Washington in 1929 while the Universalist National Memorial Church was under construction. Universalists had struggled to maintain a viable congregation in Washington, removed from Universalism's areas of strength in small towns of the Midwest and the Northeast. For some, creating the National Memorial Church in Washington would confirm Universalism's status as a denomination with a nationwide presence. For others, it was a waste of money that could have been better used to support local congregations, establish a viable pension program for ministers, or create program resources that would attract a new generation to Universalism. In this photograph, delegates to the Universalist General Convention pose on the White House lawn with Pres. Herbert Hoover. (UNMC.)

Four

A CATHEDRAL CHURCH FOR UNIVERSALISTS

What was happening with the Universalists during the early 20th century, when the Unitarians were so active and visible?

Washington did not provide an environment where a Universalist church would naturally thrive. It was located apart from Universalism's primary constituencies in the Midwest and the Northeast. The population of the city was largely transient because those serving in government positions lived for a time in the capital city and then moved on. And those from small towns and rural areas—the base of Universalism's population—did not often venture into Washington.

Furthermore, Universalism was entering a period of membership decline nationally. In the mid-19th century, Universalists had claimed several hundred thousand members. By the beginning of the 20th century, that number had shrunk to about 45,000. Partially this was due to a weak central organization that did not have sufficient resources to promote growth. But also the central message of Universalism became less distinctive. When other churches focused on frightening people about the torments of eternal damnation, Universalism offered a fresh and hopeful message. But as the nation matured, churches became less concerned with the fires of hell, thereby undercutting the uniqueness of the Universalist faith.

And yet, the dream of a national Universalist church in Washington continued to burn bright among many denominational leaders. Writing in 1905, the minister of Washington's local Universalist church, John van Schaik, articulated his dream of a national Universalist church, "Here a church would be like a city set upon a hill, the light of which could not be hid."

Despite limited resources, a campaign began to raise funds to build the long-delayed cathedral church in Washington. Universalists nationwide purchased building stones, and children contributed pennies. The time had finally come, and even the Depression did not halt the project. When the Universalist National Memorial Church was dedicated in 1930, there was a sense of accomplishment and deep pride among Universalists. It was, as one speaker put it, "the fruition of a long, long dream."

The Universalist presence in Washington, D.C., was quieter than that of the Unitarians. They did not attract the cast of local and national leaders that the Unitarians did. Rather, the church served its membership with the distinctive message of a loving God desiring redemption for all His people, a God for whom no soul was forever lost. This photograph dates from 1923. (UNMC.)

The idea of a Universalist National Memorial Church dates back to 1866. On a rainy day in April 1929, Universalists gathered for the cornerstone-laying ceremony to begin construction on this long-deferred dream. (UNMC.)

Why was there a push for a Universalist National Memorial Church? Backers of the plan cited several reasons. One was to honor Universalists who had served in World War I. Another was to prop up the Washington Universalist congregation, which had always been marginal. But the primary motivator was to give the Universalists a distinctive presence in the national capital. (UNMC.)

The Church of Our Father in Washington, which predated the Universalist National Memorial Church, had been without a regular minister since 1920. And so a key hurdle was passed when Frederick Perkins, who had a successful ministry in Lynn, Massachusetts, agreed to serve as minister of the Universalist National Memorial Church. Here he speaks at the cornerstone laying. (UNMC.)

The location for the new church was the corner of Sixteenth and S Streets in northwest Washington, an area of graceful townhouses and churches, which features many tree-lined streets. Showing in the background of this photograph is the headquarters of the Scottish Rite of Freemasonry, completed in 1915. (UNMC.)

The architects for the church were Francis H. Allen and Charles Collens of Boston, who also designed Rockefeller Chapel at the University of Chicago and Riverside Church in New York. The style draws from the tradition of Romanesque church architecture and uses semicircular arches, a large tower, and thick walls, conveying a sense of massiveness. (UNMC.)

The project to build a "cathedral church" for Universalists had been controversial from the start, particularly in the Midwest, where a church in Washington seemed far removed from the priorities of congregations that often struggled to survive. For some, this project would create a white elephant that would be an endless drain on resources while contributing little to maintaining a vital Universalist faith. Criticism intensified amidst cost overruns and fund-raising shortfalls, made more acute by the timing: the early years of the Great Depression. And yet, when the building was dedicated in the spring of 1930, there was among Universalists deep satisfaction in this accomplishment and the statement the church made for their faith. As had been hoped, Universalists visiting the nation's capital often included a stop at the new National Memorial Church. It became a recognizable face for the denomination. (UUA.)

The tower of the church was dedicated to ideals of international understanding and world peace. It was named in honor of Owen D. Young, a Universalist businessman and diplomat who had formulated a plan for addressing the problem of German war reparations after World War I. This was one of the first monuments to world peace in Washington. (UNMC.)

TABLET ON WORLD PEACE TOWER
UNIVERSALIST NATIONAL MEMORIAL CHURCH
WASHINGTON, D.C.

The commitment to international justice and world peace is a natural expression of the Universalist belief in a God who loves all His people. Universalists affirmed that all will be saved, that the world is not divided into those who receive God's grace and those who do not. They emphasized what unites humanity, despite the differences, not what keeps people apart. (UUA.)

The first services at the new Universalist National Memorial Church were held on Palm Sunday in April 1930. Attendance that morning was in excess of the seating capacity of 500. For the previous three years, the congregation had met at the Ambassador Theater, since the former building had already been sold. Now it was time to enter this new home. (UUA.)

MAIN ENTRANCE
UNIVERSALIST NATIONAL MEMORIAL CHURCH
WASHINGTON, DC.

The choir of the Universalist National Memorial Church, known as the National Capital Choir, was featured in a broadcast of carols on Christmas Eve 1931. The program originated at the headquarters of the National Press Club and was carried to an international audience by both the NBC and CBS radio networks. The theme of the program was "world friendliness." (UNMC.)

Ministers of the Universalist National Memorial Church had a unique relationship with the local church and the national denomination. They were called by both, and both contributed to their salaries. Pictured here are three ministers of the Universalist church in Washington. John van Schaik Jr. served the Church of our Father. Seth R. Brooks and Frederick S. Perkins served the Universalist National Memorial Church. (UNMC.)

Money to build the new church had been raised from Universalists nationwide. Symbolic building stones sold for $10 each, memorial contributions were sought, and children in Universalist churches contributed pennies to "their" new national church. The pennies so raised were designated for the pictured baptismal font. (UUA.)

The sanctuaries of the new Universalist and the new Unitarian churches—built within 10 years of each other—were quite different. All Souls Church featured simple lines with little ornamentation, recalling New England Unitarian churches. The Universalists created a space for worship rich in symbolism and clearly related to the Christian tradition as well as to the cathedrals of Europe. (UNMC.)

In 1939, Brooks was called from a successful pastorate in Malden, Massachusetts, to be minister of the Universalist National Memorial Church. Under his leadership, Universalists in Washington became energetic participants in the religious and secular life of the city. Here Brooks offers recognition on Children's Day, 1949. (UNMC.)

Universalists and Unitarians entered the postwar years with a commitment to addressing human need as an important expression of their faith. The end of World War II created opportunities for service as both Europe and Japan sought to recover from the war's devastation. The Unitarian Service Committee and the Universalist Service Committee, both founded in the 1940s, often worked together. One such effort involved collecting food to feed Europeans who were facing starvation in the war's aftermath. All Souls Church kicked off the effort by collecting five tons of food in the first seven days of the campaign. In this photograph, Selma Florence Burton helps in the food collection drive. Selma was the wife of Harold H. Burton, who served as senator from Ohio and then associate justice of the Supreme Court. A Republican, Harold Burton had been nominated by Democrat Harry S Truman. On the Supreme Court, Burton played a key role in assembling the unanimous opinion on the *Brown vs. Board of Education* desegregation ruling. (ASC.)

Five

RELIGIOUS LIBERALISM POSTWAR

What did it mean to be a Unitarian or a Universalist? This question presented itself as World War II ended and religious liberals faced a changed world. Up to this time, both Unitarians and Universalists had viewed themselves in relationship with the American Protestant tradition. But now, questions were raised whether they could prosper—or even survive—if either lapsed into being "just another Protestant denomination."

The Universalist Church of America had been invited to be part of the Federal Council of the Churches of Christ in America (a precursor to the National Council of Churches). In 1944, the Universalists made a formal application for membership but were rejected. No reason was given for the decision, but those who opposed the application indicated they might change their minds if the Universalists adopted a formal statement accepting Jesus Christ as "Divine Lord and Savior." While those Universalists with strong ties to the Christian tradition were disappointed, others took this as encouragement to develop a Universalist faith that reached beyond Christianity to a world faith that sought to unite seekers of different beliefs and traditions.

On the Unitarian side, a new generation of leaders sought to rethink the identity and message of religious liberalism. Key among these was the new minister called to All Souls Church in 1944, A. Powell Davies. Davies advocated a faith characterized by a rationalist worldview, involvement in social justice concerns, and the evolution toward a universal world faith. He articulated his understanding of what it was to be a Unitarian in this new age: "Unitarian churches are founded on individual freedom of belief, discipleship to advancing truth, the democratic process in human relationship, universal brotherhood, undivided by nation, race or creed, and allegiance to the cause of a united world community."

This intellectual ferment on both the Unitarian and Universalist sides—and a new identity for religious liberals that formed—anticipated the biggest surge of growth yet experienced in either tradition.

"He spoke quietly, with a Welsh brogue," one member recalled, "and though the sanctuary was packed, everyone listened so intently that you could hear a pin drop." In May 1944, A. Powell Davies was called to be minister of All Souls Church in Washington. He advocated a vital religious liberalism that brought dramatic changes to All Souls Church, to Unitarians in the Washington region, and to religious liberalism nationally. Davies had grown up in England of Welsh parents. He began his career as a Methodist minister in England but was drawn to the United States in search of greater religious freedom. While serving Methodist churches in Maine, he encountered American Unitarianism and was convinced that this was his true religious home. In 1933, Davies changed his affiliation to become a Unitarian minister. (ASC.)

Before coming to Washington, Davies was minister of the Community Church of Summit, New Jersey where he became a forceful voice among Unitarians. He advocated that the church become involved in activism for social change. Among his causes was family planning, and Davies was among the first religious leaders to support the work of Planned Parenthood. (ASC.)

Davies envisioned a new identity for American Unitarianism. Many years before, William Ellery Channing had called for a "Universal Church." Davies now advocated a universal faith that reached beyond the confines of Christianity. Here he speaks at a service commemorating the 100th anniversary of the birth of William Howard Taft. (ASC.)

The Charmian Club was the Unitarian youth group at All Souls Church, the precursor to later youth groups that developed among the Washington Unitarian and Unitarian Universalist churches. Its aims were to foster connections among young people of the church as well as to encourage consideration of what it meant to be a young religious liberal. This photograph dates from 1941. (ASC.)

As is typical among youth groups of long standing, many informal rituals developed. There was an annual gathering during Labor Day weekend in Pennsylvania at an inn located near the Catoctin Mountains. The expectation was that participants stay up all night for both nights of the outing, a tradition which the youth ministers who accompanied them found challenging, at best. (ASC.)

When the Harvard Street church was dedicated, the space under the sanctuary was left unfinished. An anonymous donor offered a contribution to All Souls Church to support its programs of community service. The result was this gymnasium, which hosted a variety of activities. This photograph of a youth group dance was taken in 1952. (ASC.)

Unitarian churches reconceived traditional religious ceremonies with contemporary meanings. The rite of baptism, understood as a cleansing of the sin of the world, became a "dedication," introducing a child, pledging support for his or her care. Here A. Powell Davies is shown with Ron Perlik at his dedication on May 16, 1954. Also shown are his parents, Annabel and Bill Perlik. (Courtesy Annabel Perlik.)

Thanks to the Unitarian Service Committee

Unitarians and Universalists responded to the dislocations of World War II by forming service committees to help with relief efforts in Europe. The photograph is from one of the homes for displaced children in Germany run by the Unitarian Service Committee. The service committees of the Unitarians and the Universalists worked together on several projects, anticipating the Unitarian Universalist merger. (ASC.)

Starting in 1937, All Souls Church provided facilities without charge for the Metropolitan Police Boys' Club, an organization offering activities for neighborhood boys. By the 1950s, there were 1,900 members, with more than 400 people participating in its activities each day. This photograph shows the Boys' Club football team watching a basketball game in the All Souls Recreation Center in 1952. (ASC.)

By the early 1950s, most activities at All Souls Church were integrated, and participation of African Americans in children's programs was increasing. An exception was the Police Boys' Club, which remained all white. After the 1954 Supreme Court decision outlawing segregation, the church board asked that the Metropolitan Police Boys' Club be integrated. (ASC.)

The Metropolitan Police Boys' Club refused to integrate and chose instead to leave the All Souls Church facilities. In response, the church organized a new boys' club—the Columbia Heights Boys Club—which would be open to all. The Unitarian Service Committee provided funding to enable this new organization to provide services to its members. (ASC.)

Throughout much of its history, Washington was a segregated city. But there were exceptions. The African American leader Frederick Douglass attended All Souls Church while Clay MacCauley was minister. And the church was among the few institutions that allowed integrated groups to meet. This 1947 photograph is of a community vacation school sponsored by the Friends Meeting of Washington in cooperation with All Souls Church. (ASC.)

A. Powell Davies took a leadership role in efforts to address the injustice of racism. In 1953, he pledged not to patronize any restaurant or entertainment venue that was closed to African Americans. He urged that others do the same and published a list of nonsegregated facilities—more than 40,000 copies were distributed throughout the Washington area. (ASC.)

April 13, 1947, was the 204th anniversary of the birth of Thomas Jefferson, an outspoken advocate of religious freedom. On that day, Washington Unitarians gathered for their Sunday service at the Jefferson Memorial. Here Frederick May Eliot, president of the American Unitarian Association, presents the sermon entitled, "What Kind of Christian was Thomas Jefferson?" (ASC.)

During the Jefferson Memorial Service, Congressman Angier Louis Goodwin of Massachusetts read from the *Jefferson Bible*, which Thomas Jefferson had created by removing sections from the Gospel stories he believed not consistent with reason. The president of the All Souls Church youth group, the Charmian Club, laid a wreath at the foot of the Jefferson statue on behalf of America's Unitarian youth. (ASC.)

The pictures on these two pages were drawn by Japanese children in Hiroshima and sent as gifts to the children of All Souls Church. A. Powell Davies was deeply troubled when atomic bombs were used at the end of World War II, and he was outraged at reports of a party at which American military officers celebrated with a three-foot angel food cake shaped like the atomic cloud that appeared over Hiroshima. (ASC.)

In 1946, Davies delivered a sermon entitled, "Lest the Living Forget," in which he expressed anger at the party featuring the atomic cloud cake and the insensitivity to human suffering he felt it represented. A copy of that sermon reached Dr. Howard Bell, an aide to Gen. Douglas MacArthur. At the time, General MacArthur supervised the postwar occupation of Japan. (ASC.)

Howard Bell wrote to Davies, describing the circumstances of 400 Japanese children from Hiroshima who lacked the most basic supplies for their studies. He asked for help in cultivating contact and understanding between American and Japanese children. In response, Davies preached another sermon advocating assistance from America's children to their counterparts in Japan. (ASC.)

The children of All Souls Church collected 1.5 tons of school supplies, which the Unitarian Service Committee sent to children in Japan. Later the Japanese children sent their thanks in the form of letters and art projects, including 48 watercolor paintings and crayon drawings. These have been displayed throughout the United States with their message that those who have been enemies can become friends. (ASC.)

In 1947, the Unitarian General Conference was held in Washington, and church leaders posed on the White House lawn with Pres. Harry S Truman. Included in this photograph are many who were or would become national Unitarian leaders. From left to right are Curtis W. Reese, Homer Jack, Clay Burkholder, Samuel A. Towne, Robert Killam, Raymond B. Bragg, Wallace Robbins, Lowell Mason, Dwight Strong, David Parke, Margot Pieksen, Thaddeus Clark, Dale DeWitt, Melvin Arnold, President Truman, Dana Greeley, Lawrence G. Brooks, A. Powell Davies, Everett M. Baker, Laurence Staples, Frederick May Eliot, Alfred W. Montzka, and Winifred Overholser. This photograph makes it obvious that in the 1940s, leadership in Unitarianism was largely a men's game. Universalists had first ordained a woman as minister in 1863, when Olympia Brown was so recognized. Celia Burleigh had been the first woman ordained as a Unitarian, in 1871. But acceptance of women as ministers came slowly. (ASC.)

In 1952, Bess Truman (left), wife of President Truman, paid a visit to the "Unitarian Bazaar" at All Souls Church. It can be assumed that this appearance did not simply reflect Bess's interest in church bazaars. It was also an indication of the political clout enjoyed by Unitarians at the time. (ASC.)

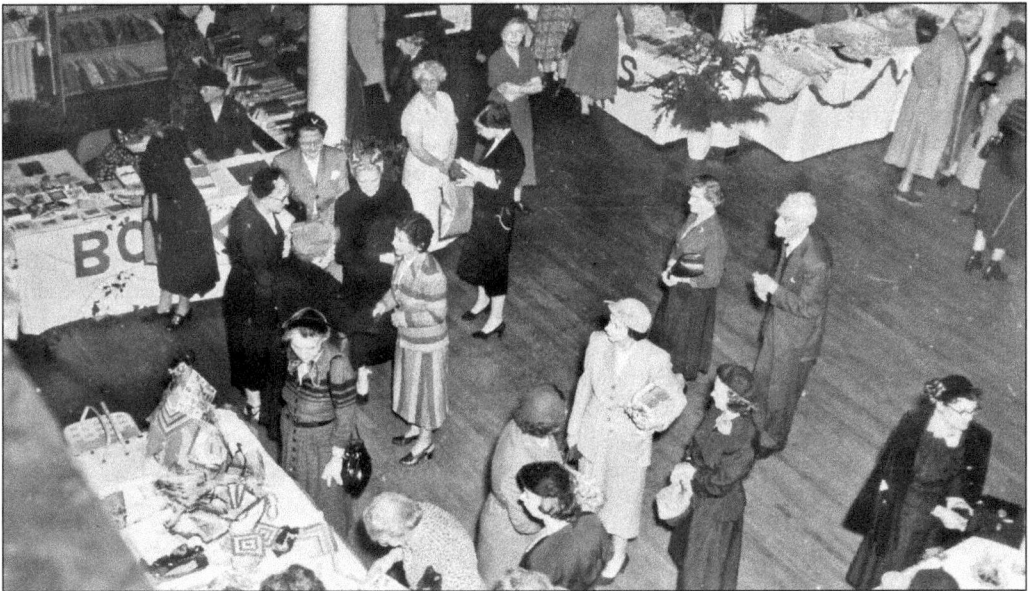

As the 1950s began, religious liberalism was poised to make changes. Davies had helped formulate a new identity and vision for Unitarianism. He suggested, "We could be forerunners of a church which includes the whole human community . . . on the basis of universal fellowship and universal freedom." Now it was time to make good on that vision. (ASC.)

In the 1950s, Washington was ripe for Unitarian and Universalist growth into the suburbs. All Souls Church was filled to overflowing; there simply was not room for all who wanted to attend. Religious liberalism was appealing to a segment of the population who sought a faith that spoke to the modern age. The baby boom produced an unprecedented demand for children's religious education. And the rush to the suburbs brought the desire for liberal churches that would be close by. In response, new Unitarian and Universalist congregations were established in the suburbs that ringed Washington. Here A. Powell Davies speaks at the ground-breaking ceremony for the new Cedar Lane Unitarian Church in Bethesda, Maryland, which was held on February 10, 1957. Also featured in this photograph is Lewis Lapham, the church's chairman of the board. (CLUUC.)

Six

GROWING INTO THE SUBURBS

To get a seat at All Souls Church on a Sunday morning when A. Powell Davies spoke, one had to get there early—maybe an hour, maybe two. Finding a parking spot in the urban neighborhood where the church was located presented a challenge. But securing a place to sit once at the church was even more difficult. Those not fortunate enough to obtain one of the coveted spots in the sanctuary were ushered to another room, possibly the Social Hall, where loudspeakers broadcast the service. But even with these difficulties, people kept coming.

This was a time when Unitarianism in Washington secured unprecedented influence. On any Sunday, the congregation might include congressmen, senators, or government officials. Three Supreme Court justices regularly attended: William O. Douglas, Hugo Black, and Harold H. Burton. Washington newspapers assigned reporters to cover the sermons given by Davies; what was said on Sunday morning at All Souls Church often appeared in Washington newspapers on Monday.

In the late 1940s and early 1950s, church attendance throughout the United States surged. The suburbs were booming as urban residents moved out of the cities to buy their own homes and establish families. In response, All Souls Church started a process of "planting" new congregations in the suburban communities that surround Washington. The Universalists also enjoyed revived prospects, and they established their own extension congregation: the Silver Spring–Takoma Park Universalist Fellowship in the Maryland suburbs.

It was a heady time. Those who remember speak of the excitement it held for religious liberalism, with new families crowding the suburban congregations. But America's move to the suburbs was a complex mixture of reaching toward possibilities and flight from challenges. As middle class families moved out, the cities became poorer, less diverse, and more dangerous. American society became more polarized. Later the underside of post–World War II growth would present new challenges for secular and religious communities alike.

For its first 125 years, Unitarianism in the Washington area was represented by only one church. A few attempts had been made to establish a second Unitarian congregation, but these did not get past the planning stages. Now new opportunities presented themselves. In this 1959 photograph, representatives from eight Unitarian congregations founded with help from All Souls Church meet together. (ASC.)

The first suburban congregations met in rental quarters, where members came to listen to a live service broadcast from All Souls Church. As unappealing as this may sound, it offered an alternative to the overcrowded downtown church while still providing the opportunity to hear A. Powell Davies. This 1951 photograph shows the Chevy Chase Women's Club, which provided space for Unitarians in Montgomery County, Maryland. (ASC.)

The suburban outreach was supported by All Souls Church through encouraging those living in targeted areas to transfer their memberships. The "mother church" also contributed money to the new churches. Here a check for $5,000 for the building fund of the Unitarian church in Arlington, Virginia, is presented. Pictured from left to right are Laurence Staples, A. Powell Davies, Carl Gibboney, and Ross Weston. (UUA.)

The first Unitarian church in suburban Washington was in Arlington, where efforts began in 1943. Initially services were held in a community center on Sunday afternoons, enabling members to attend All Souls Church in the morning. In 1947, Gilbert A. Phillips was installed as associate minister at All Souls Church with a special responsibility for working with the new Arlington church. (UUA.)

The Arlington church grew rapidly. Within a year after Gilbert Phillips was installed with shared responsibilities at All Souls Church, he became full time at Arlington. By 1948, the church registered a membership of 117, with a church school enrollment of 103. This photograph shows members of the Unitarian Church of Arlington planning a dinner to support the church building fund. (UUA.)

As was the case with many suburban Unitarian churches, the Arlington congregation led a peripatetic existence in its early years, moving from place to place as circumstances dictated. After meeting for worship in such venues as the Buckingham Community Room, the Ashton Heights Women's Club, and the Kate Waller Barrett School, ground was broken for its own building in November 1948. (UUA.)

Even with their own buildings, services in Unitarian churches of the 1950s were often informal, with worship held in multipurpose rooms. Sanctuaries were designed to accommodate Sunday services, fellowship dinners, children's plays, and events by outside community groups; folding chairs became as essential to church as pews had been to previous generations. This picture dates from 1957 at the Unitarian Church of Arlington. (UUA.)

An essential part of the ritual of church in new suburban congregations was the coffee hour, held after services were completed. Here people met each other, caught up on news of the community, and made personal and professional contacts. Coffee was the lifeblood of the Unitarian community during the 1950s. (UUA.)

A similar scenario to that of Arlington played out as Unitarians established churches throughout the Washington suburbs. This photograph is of the first congregational meeting of the Unitarian Church of Montgomery County, held at the Chevy Chase Women's Club on March 8, 1953. At this meeting, those gathered voted to organize themselves into the Unitarian Church of Montgomery County. (CLUUC.)

As with Arlington Unitarians, the Montgomery County congregation met in rented facilities while looking for a location of its own. A 6-acre wooded site on Cedar Lane in Bethesda was purchased, and planning commenced for a building. In this 1956 photograph, the teen group of the Montgomery County Unitarians wields machetes to clear a space for the ground-breaking ceremony. (CLUUC.)

If All Souls Church was the "mother church" for the newly established Unitarian congregations, A. Powell Davies was their father. Many suburban residents were reluctant to cut their ties to the parents and devote themselves primarily to the new local churches. So Davies made himself available for such occasions as this ground-breaking for the Unitarian Church of Montgomery County. (CLUUC.)

In reference to its new location, the Unitarian Church of Montgomery County changed its name to Cedar Lane Unitarian Church. The new building, gently set on its wooded property, won several awards, including one from the American Institute of Architects for its relationship to the natural surroundings. This photograph was taken in 1958. (CLUUC.)

Universalists also reached into the Washington suburbs, establishing the Silver Spring–Takoma Park (Maryland) Universalist Fellowship in 1952. In this 1954 photograph, members gather in the converted stable on the property they purchased after originally meeting at Hillandale Elementary School. Meetings were held in that stable until other facilities were built. The stable still stands and continues to be used by the congregation. (UUA.)

The Silver Spring congregation was the last established by the Universalists before merging with the Unitarians in 1961. This church was also the first to use both "Unitarian" and "Universalist" in its name. It is currently known as the Unitarian Universalist Church of Silver Spring. In this 1953 photograph, members go to work on the driveway of their new property. (UUA.)

The story of a new congregation often features unexpected problems and setbacks, along with the accomplishments. Here members of the Paint Branch Unitarian Church pose by a stack of tires that someone dumped on their newly purchased property. More typical challenges involve the necessity of raising sufficient money to fund the dreams of a new church. (PBUUC.)

When cash is short—and it always is in a new congregation—members offer their labor to help bridge the gap between what the church needs and what the church can afford. Hence is the centrality of what is described by the oxymoron, "work party." Looking back, members often recall both the hard work and the deep satisfaction that came with starting a church. (PBUUC.)

An important factor driving the expansion of Unitarianism into the Washington suburbs was the post–World War II baby boom. People were starting families, buying homes, enrolling their children in schools, and seeking religious education. This photograph shows Family Sunday at the Unitarian Church of Montgomery County in 1953, then meeting at the Chevy Chase Women's Club. (CLUUC.)

In its planning, the Unitarian Church of Montgomery County anticipated that there would be 58 children in its religious education program. In fact, the number was much higher. On the first day, 170 children attended, with others joining later. The church went to double Sunday sessions to accommodate the number of families that were turning up. (CLUUC.)

Unitarian churches were surprised and unprepared for the influx of children they experienced in the 1950s. They did not have the facilities or volunteer staffing to meet the demand. In this photograph, children of the Unitarian Church of Montgomery County, Maryland, meet for religious education in a cloakroom. (CLUUC.)

If a cloakroom was not available, a class might meet in a hallway, as in this photograph. What was the appeal that brought families to Unitarian churches? At the center was an effort to rethink the nature of religious education. Rather than indoctrination, the aim was to help children grow into adults who could make their own decisions in religion—and in life. (CLUUC.)

During the ministry of A. Powell Davies, the Sunday school was renamed the School of Religion. The meaning behind the change was that children would learn about religion: their own and those of their neighbors and those of the world. With greater knowledge, it was hoped, would come understanding and sympathy for people of other faiths, for people who were different. (ASC.)

A goal in the ministry of Davies was to bridge gaps in understanding and sympathy that keep people apart. "How strange and foolish," he wrote, "are these walls of understanding that divide us." Unitarian religious education sought to give children the skills necessary to grow into adults who might help build community. (ASC.)

In this mural, created by Kathleen Bruskin for the Unitarian Church of Arlington, the symbols of the world religions are featured, suggesting an openness to the truths of all these traditions. On the Universalist side at this same time, some were reaching beyond its primary identification with Christianity and toward a more inclusive world faith. (UUA.)

Sophia Lyon Fahs was a pioneer in religious education who grew up as an evangelical Christian. Her views liberalized in response to progressive educational theory, and in 1937, she was hired by the American Unitarian Association to develop a new children's curriculum. This photograph shows her 1959 ordination as a minister by Cedar Lane Unitarian Church in Bethesda, which then claimed more than 800 children in its program. (CLUUC.)

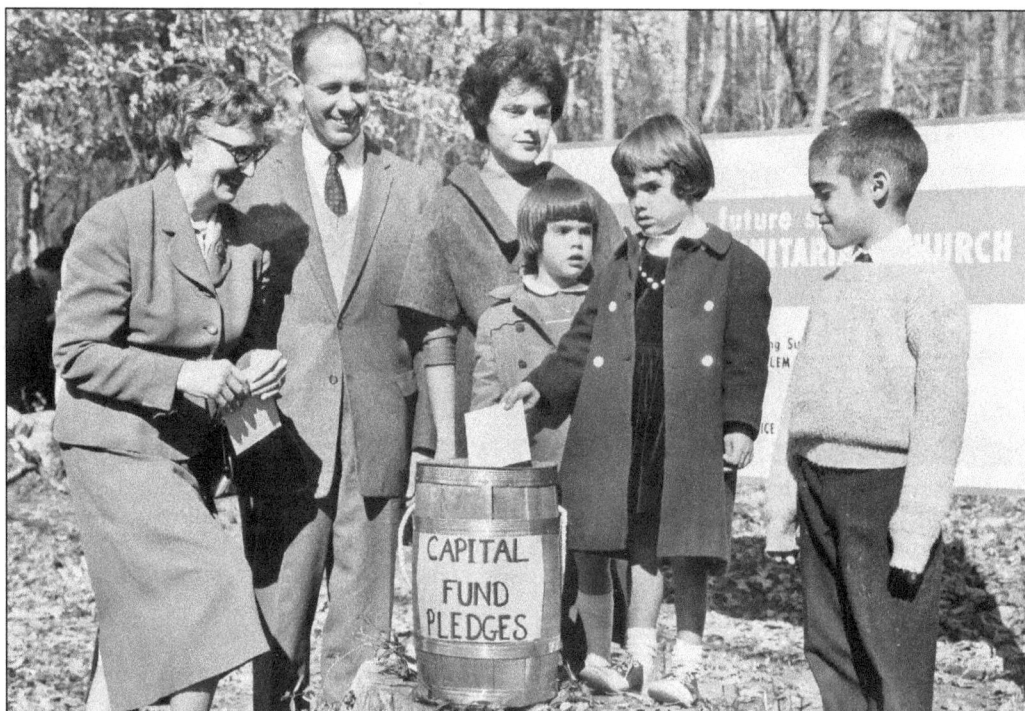

A newly established congregation would initially meet in rented quarters. Then a drive to raise money for a building commenced. The River Road Unitarian Church in Bethesda was sponsored by the Cedar Lane Unitarian Church (which had itself been sponsored by All Souls Church). Pictured from left to right are Muriel Davies, Dale Button, JoEllen Lobo, and her children promoting the campaign for the new congregation's building. (RRUUC.)

The new church secured property, hired an architect, and began designing and building facilities to serve its fledgling congregation. On June 14, 1964, members of the River Road Unitarian Church gathered for the ceremonial beginning of construction. In this photograph, the congregation's minister, Bob Lewis, speaks through the megaphone. (RRUUC.)

At the ground-breaking ceremony for the River Road Unitarian Church, participants joined hands and stood around the new building's perimeter. Participant Brad Patterson remembered, "By holding hands where the walls would be, we symbolized what our church would be: all of us together as a congregation." (RRUUC.)

In this 1964 photograph, taken of the River Road Unitarian Church ground-breaking, the congregation is visible from the road on the site of the new church. This building was not created without conflict. The necessity of taking down some trees created one controversy; ribbons reading "over my dead body" were wrapped around those destined to be removed. (RRUUC.)

Church buildings make statements about the values of a congregation. The suburban Washington Unitarian churches sought to create facilities that honored the simplicity of the Unitarian architectural tradition, an openness to diversity, the love of nature and the natural environment, and a functionality that enabled churches to sponsor a variety of activities. (RRUUC.)

The River Road Unitarian Church was dedicated in 1965. In 1966, it was named by the American Institute of Architects as one of the 10 best buildings of the year. The jury award praised this "handsomely unpretentious building which expresses the Unitarian philosophy with clarity and vigor . . . It achieves crisp simplicity and effortless variety, and its rapport with its wooded site is thoroughly pleasing." (RRUUC.)

Sanctuaries created for Unitarian congregations in the 1950s and 1960s adhered to the tradition of unadorned worship space made more inviting with the use of light and wood. One goal was to create a place of worship that would be welcoming to those of many religious backgrounds. This photograph shows the completed sanctuary at the River Road Unitarian Church. (RRUUC.)

In 1954, the College Park Unitarian Center was established. Sunday services followed a pattern in which the congregation sang hymns and shared readings. Then, when A. Powell Davies started his sermon, a telephone call linked to All Souls Church in Washington, and the sermon would be broadcast to the congregation. The College Park Unitarians later moved to Adelphi as the Paint Branch Unitarian Church, shown here. (PBUUC.)

The plan to establish Unitarian congregations in the Washington suburbs, which began at All Souls Church in the early 1940s, yielded eight new Unitarian congregations by 1959. The congregation in Arlington was the first. It was followed by the Cedar Lane Unitarian Church in Bethesda and the Mount Vernon Unitarian Church, both established in 1953. This photograph is of the Unitarian Church of Arlington. (UUA.)

All Souls Church founded the Unitarian Church of Arlington. Then the congregation at Arlington established the Unitarian Church at Fairfax in Oakton, Virginia (shown here). The churches built by the Washington-area Unitarian congregations were resolutely modern, differing from the more traditional architecture of All Souls Church and in dramatic contrast to the cathedral architecture of the Universalist National Memorial Church. (UUCF.)

In 1953, All Souls Church started a congregation to serve southeast Washington, D.C., and Prince George's County, Maryland. Originally named the Southeast Unitarian Center, it became Davies Memorial Unitarian Church in honor of A. Powell Davies, who had recently died. Located in a less affluent section than other suburban Washington congregations, Davies became a model for diversity in its membership. (DMUUC.)

Suburban Washington Unitarian congregations showed a proclivity for placing their churches among trees. Most feature interior views that mask the fact that they are located in densely populated areas, possibly a nod to the nature mysticism of early Unitarians Ralph Waldo Emerson and Henry David Thoreau. Pictured here is the Unitarian church located in Rockville. (UUA.)

Here the first minister of River Road Unitarian Church, Bob Lewis, performs the dedication rite at the congregation's temporary quarters before constructing its own building. The pathway from start-up congregation to established church always held its surprises and challenges. But the suburban outreach of All Souls Church has proven uncommonly successful in creating viable congregations of the liberal religious tradition. (RRUUC.)

Why did Unitarian churches of the 1950s grow so dramatically? One reason was that it was a time of growth throughout American Protestant churches. Another reason was that Unitarianism offered a spirituality that spoke uniquely to the new age. But "white flight" also contributed. As white liberals fled the city, they moved to suburban Unitarian churches where issues of race were more comfortably distant. (PBUUC.)

This notice was sent to announce the sudden death of A. Powell Davies on September 27, 1957, at age 55. Unitarians nationwide were stunned at his loss. Less than five months later, on February 18, 1958, Frederick May Eliot, president of the American Unitarian Association, also died. Two architects of the dynamic Unitarian growth of the 1940s and 1950s were gone. (CLUUC.)

Despite the loss of these two preeminent leaders, the groundwork for future growth had been laid. This chart, which appeared in the All Souls Church newsletter, graphed the increase in Washington-area Unitarianism. Adult membership almost quadrupled from 900 in 1944 to 3,470 in 1958. Enrollment in children's religious education increased by a factor of 10, from just over 200 to almost 2,300. (ASC.)

AMERICAN UNITARIAN ASSOCIATION
BOSTON MASSACHUSETTS

OFFICE OF THE PRESIDENT

September 27, 1957

Dear Colleague,

Powell Davies, minister of All Souls Unitarian Church, Washington, D.C., died yesterday in his 56th year. This sudden loss will affect us all, for all of us felt the influence of his courageous and eloquent spirit. He epitomized "Unitarian Advance"; and as we continue going forward together, he will not be forgotten.

Faithfully yours,
Frederick May Eliot.

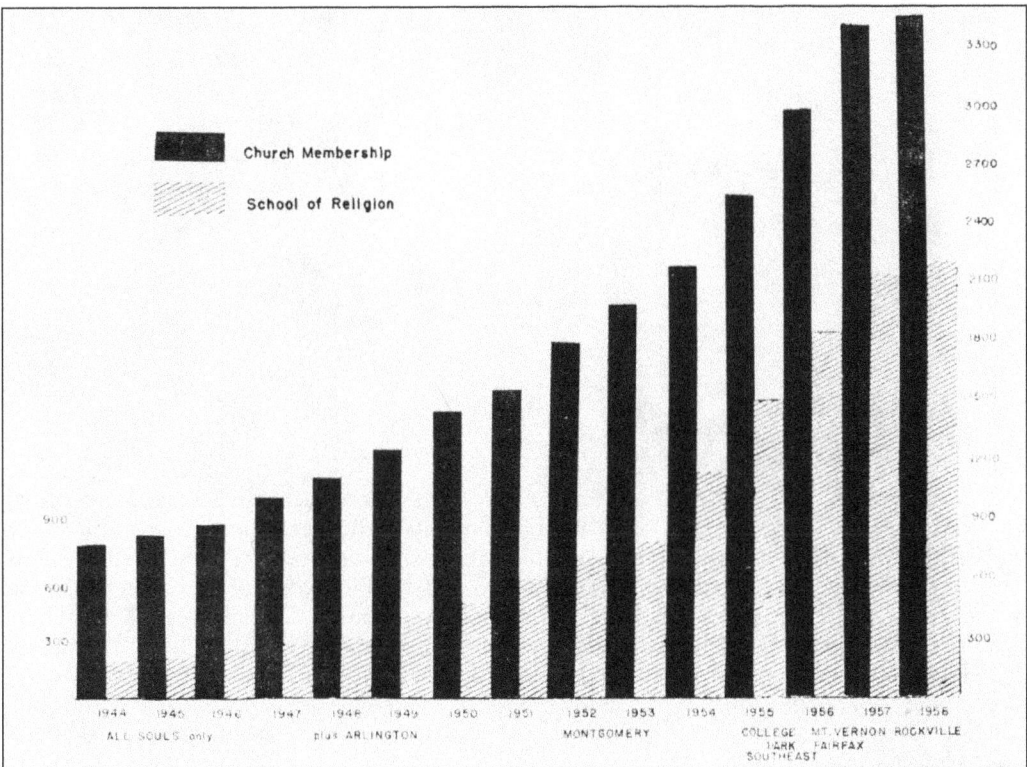

On March 28, 1963, almost 1,000 Unitarian Universalists gathered to participate in the March on Washington for Jobs and Freedom. Some spent the night before on cots at All Souls Church. The total crowd was estimated at between 200,000 and 300,000, and featured speeches by the major civil rights leaders from the steps of the Lincoln Memorial. The civil rights movement galvanized the newly formed Unitarian Universalist Association. Even though the Unitarians and Universalists had separate histories, they shared the values of affirming human rights, equal justice, and equal opportunity for all. Shown here are marchers gathering outside of All Souls Church before boarding buses for the Mall, where participants heard Martin Luther King Jr. give his "I Have a Dream" speech. (ASC.)

Seven

Unitarians and Universalists Unite

Thomas Starr King, who served the First Unitarian Church of San Francisco during the Civil War years, held standing as both a Unitarian and a Universalist minister. When asked why the two liberal denominations did not merge, he speculated that perhaps Unitarians and Universalists were "too near of kin to be married."

Indeed, the similarities were striking. Both affirmed religious freedom, both were non-creedal, both looked to a God of love and a human Jesus, both sought to express their ideals in the larger community. Throughout the 19th century and into the 20th century, the possibility of joining forces was often raised, but serious efforts at merger did not occur.

The hesitance stemmed less from theological than social and stylistic differences. Unitarians drew mostly from urban and educated populations, while Universalists were more likely to be from small towns and rural areas. The style of worship also differed, with Universalists favoring a more emotional approach to faith than the famously rational Unitarians. So while Unitarians and Universalist could not find much to disagree about on religious issues, they still viewed each other cautiously.

In Washington, All Souls Church and the Universalist National Memorial Church cooperated in some realms. Summer services combined the Universalist and Unitarian congregations along with a liberal Congregational church. Youth meetings and discussion groups were also jointly sponsored. But there was wariness too. The ministers of the Universalist National Memorial Church and All Souls Church both opposed joining of the two associations of congregations. The Universalist, Seth R. Brooks, was concerned that Universalism would be overshadowed by the Unitarians and lose its Christian focus. The Unitarian, A. Powell Davies, worried that the more conservative Universalists would resist creating the progressive liberal faith he envisioned.

Yet when the merger of the two associations was completed in 1961, the Universalist Church of Silver Spring, Maryland, had a sign already waiting. Upon hearing that the union was official, they became the first local congregation in the nation to claim the new name: the Unitarian Universalist Church of Silver Spring.

The possibility of joining Unitarians and Universalists was often suggested, but both sides resisted. Thomas Starr King summarized the difference between the two in an often-quoted remark. He said that the Universalists thought that God was too good to damn them forever, while the Unitarians thought they were too good to be damned. Pictured here is early Unitarian leader William Ellery Channing. (ASC.)

Efforts to join the two movements became serious after World War II. One reason was the rejection of Universalists by the Federal Council of the Churches of Christ. Another was a decline in membership in Universalist churches. But there was also the vision of a united church, bringing religious liberals together. In May 1961, the Unitarian Universalist Association was formed. Pictured here is early Universalist leader John Murray. (ASC.)

Even before merging their organizations, Unitarians and Universalists had joined in calling for a religious faith that reached across national and denominational boundaries: a religion for one world. This photograph shows representatives to the May 1959 meeting of the International Association for Liberal Christianity and Religious Freedom. Pictured from left to right are Dana McLean Greeley, H. Stewart Carter, Edward A. Cahill, and Ernest W. Kuebler. (ASC.)

The Unitarian Service Committee was established in 1940 as an agency of humanitarian aid. The Universalist Service Committee was formed after World War II with similar aims. The two service committees cooperated in shared projects, anticipating the merger of the Unitarian and the Universalists. This photograph shows a service committee program in Cambodia. (ASC.)

After the death of A. Powell Davies, a national search was conducted to find a new minister for All Souls Church. The candidate chosen was Duncan Howlett, then minister of First Church in Boston. He assumed his post in 1958, at the beginning of a time of dramatic transition both for the nation and for the new Unitarian Universalist Association. In this photograph, Howlett greets Margaret Lee. (ASC.)

These were exciting times. Unitarianism was expanding rapidly into the Washington suburbs, and church members exerted leadership in both public and private realms. In a letter to the All Souls Church congregation, the board chairman wrote, "It is becoming clear that we are at the center of a great religious movement that can powerfully affect . . . the policy and course of our government." This picture shows Elizabeth Kittredge and Howlett. (ASC.)

Howlett continued the tradition of Unitarian involvement in social concerns by addressing such issues as civil rights, the war on poverty, family planning, the war in Vietnam, and home rule for the District of Columbia. A lawyer before entering the ministry, he was able to address ethical and societal issues from both legal and theological perspectives. After the 1963 March on Washington, Howlett reflected, "Some six hundred of us came for a briefing, remained for a service of dedication to the cause of human liberty, and departed for the Washington Monument . . . As we crossed Constitution Avenue and looked toward the Monument, there was an audible gasp of delight as we saw that the whole hillside . . . was crowded with people." (ASC.)

In 1959, James Reeb became assistant minister of All Souls Church, where he became deeply involved in community issues. After serving for five years, he resigned to devote himself full time to work as a civil rights activist. In 1965, Reeb went to Alabama to join the March on Selma in response to a call to clergy from Martin Luther King Jr. (ASC.)

In Selma, Reeb and two other Unitarian Universalist ministers were attacked and beaten; Reeb died from his injuries. Pres. Lyndon B. Johnson, then preparing the Voting Rights Act, was moved by the tragedy. Public sympathy for this clergyman who sacrificed his life was an important factor in convincing Congress to pass voting rights legislation. Here he is pictured at All Souls Church. (ASC.)

Martin Luther King Jr. gave the eulogy at the memorial service for Reeb at Brown Chapel in Selma, Alabama on March 15, 1965. King observed, "His death was the result of a sensitive religious spirit. His crime was that he dared live his faith; he placed himself alongside the disinherited black brethren of his community." (ASC.)

Suburban Unitarian congregations also became involved in the civil rights movement, seeking to end segregation in their communities as well as participating in efforts to influence local and national legislation. This 1956 photograph shows an integrated Brownie troop that was sponsored by the Unitarian Church of Fairfax in Oakton. (UUCF.)

Duncan Howlett retired from his ministry at All Souls Church in 1968 and recommended that the church call an African American minister to replace him. At the time, no African American had ever served as senior minister of a large Unitarian Universalist congregation. The congregation called David Eaton, shown here near a bust of A. Powell Davies. (*Unitarian Universalist Association Inactive Minister Files, 1825-1999,* bMS 1446, AHTL.)

As a student, Eaton was attracted to religious liberalism but had been discouraged from becoming a minister by both Unitarians and Universalists. Instead, he entered the Methodist ministry. When called as senior minister of All Souls Church, he retained his Methodist affiliation. Eaton believed that "the primary purpose [of the church] is to help people discover, create, and maintain hope in their lives." (ASC.)

With Eaton as minister, All Souls Church became a center of activism, and Unitarian Universalist congregations throughout the Washington area participated in efforts to create a society of justice and compassion. This photograph is of the cover of a Sunday service promoting the Sanctuary Movement, which offered protection to Central Americans vulnerable to deportation because of their political activities. (ASC.)

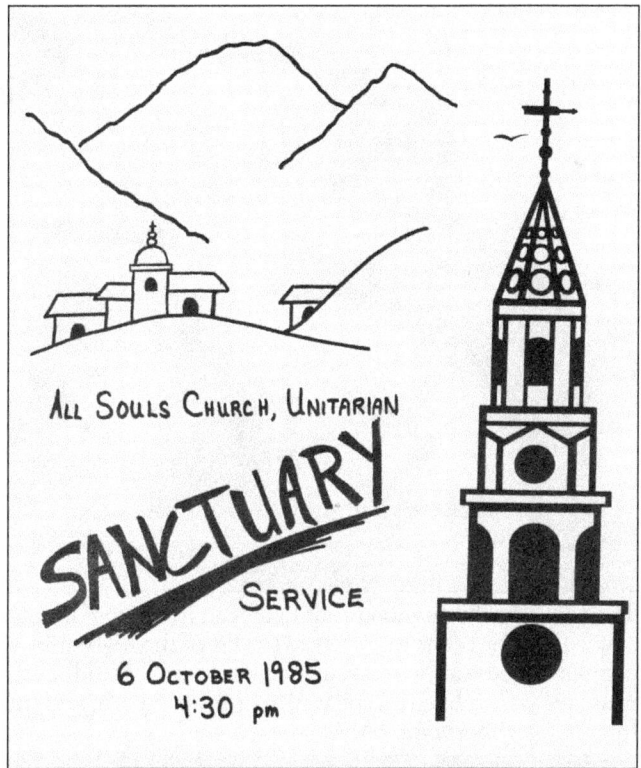

ALL SOULS CHURCH, UNITARIAN

SANCTUARY

SERVICE

6 OCTOBER 1985
4:30 pm

The struggle for social justice was often featured in Sunday worship. This photograph from the 1985 Sanctuary service includes (standing) Loretta Williams of the Unitarian Universalist Association and Eaton. Seated are a Central American who was given sanctuary by All Souls Church and a representative from the Sanctuary organization. (ASC.)

The genteel neighborhood that had been home to All Souls Church since 1922 entered a period of decline. The crime rate grew to be one of the highest in Washington, buildings were neglected, population density increased, and those who could moved to the suburbs. All Souls Church members were robbed on the way to or from church, and the congregation was becoming isolated from its neighborhood. (ASC.)

After the 1968 assassination of Martin Luther King Jr., riots caused substantial damage in the neighborhood where All Souls Church was located. Buildings burned, stores were looted, and police patrolled the streets. The hopelessness felt by many residents had turned to violence. This old Unitarian church with a history of civil debate on social issues faced a new challenge right in its own backyard. (ASC.)

Members of All Souls Church formed the All Souls Housing Corporation in 1971 to provide affordable housing for residents of the Columbia Heights section in Washington. In 1977, the corporation opened Columbia Heights Village, a 10-story high-rise with 406 units available to people of modest incomes. Since then, it has developed several other residential properties in the church neighborhood. (ASC.)

In addition to housing, church members addressed other neighborhood issues. The Girard Street Project opened a community playground, created a tutoring program, established a mother's club, sponsored block parties, helped create a credit union, lobbied legislators, and hired an executive director to oversee these programs. The overall aim was to help residents get acquainted, share concerns, and become a neighborhood. (ASC.)

With the strong social justice witness of the congregation and with David Eaton as minister, All Souls Church approached a 50/50 balance of white and African American membership, the first in the Unitarian Universalist Association to reach that level. However, most of the suburban congregations remained primarily white, often receiving memberships of white Unitarian Universalists who had fled the city of Washington. (ASC.)

Eaton's activism inspired many to become involved in actions seeking social justice. Unitarian Universalists participated in such rallies as the National Peace Action Coalition at Pres. Richard Nixon's inauguration, in the campaign to free the Wilmington 10, and in efforts to protect the most vulnerable members of American society. In this photograph, members of the Outreach Club protest Medicaid cuts in 1976. (ASC.)

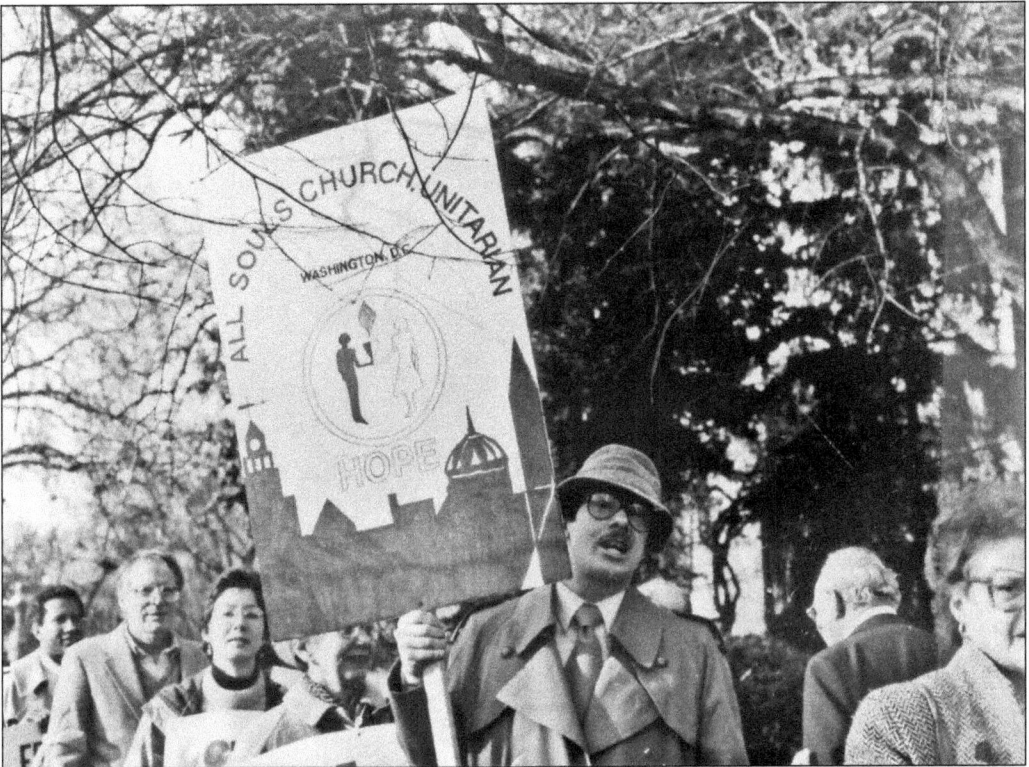

Drawing upon the historic Unitarian and Universalist emphasis on global awareness, church members reached beyond national borders and sought to understand the nation's impact upon the international community. Here demonstrators witness against the practice of apartheid, or racial separation, in South Africa. This photograph was taken at the Washington Embassy of the Republic of South Africa in 1985. (ASC.)

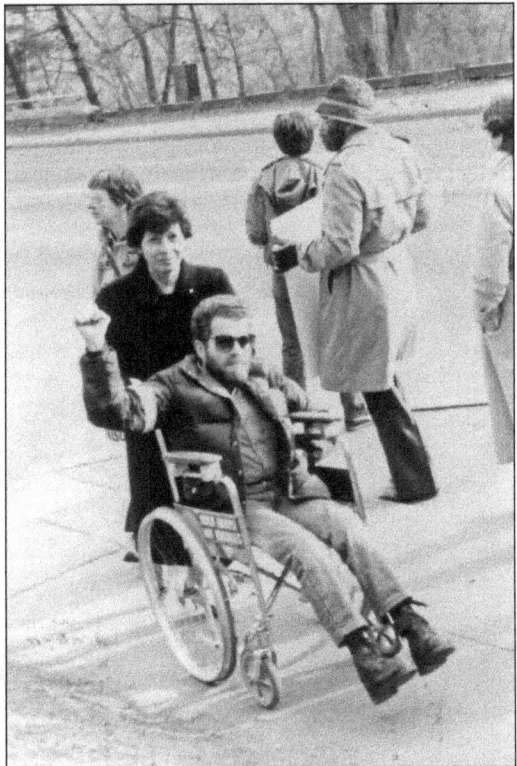

An article in the *Washington Post* about Eaton's ministry at All Souls Church noted the contrast between the activism he encouraged and the Unitarian tradition of rational inquiry: hot activism and cool skepticism. If this was not always a comfortable mix, it did produce a dynamic period in Washington Unitarian Universalism. Here Mark and Celia Sharp participate in the demonstration at the South African embassy. (ASC.)

The 1960s were a time of innovation and experimentation in the recently established suburban Unitarian Universalist congregations. Art forms such as new music, poetry, storytelling, and dance were incorporated into worship. The intent was to express the challenges and possibilities of being human. In this photograph, the minister of the Unitarian Universalist Church of Fairfax, Rudy Nemser, presides at a worship service featuring modern dance. (UUCF.)

Religious education was not confined to children. Adults also benefited from exploring values and beliefs of the world's religious traditions and considering how these applied to their own lives. Unitarian Universalist adult education addressed concerns like personal religious history and the intersection of science and religion. In this photograph, taken in 1967, Hugo Holleroth conducts a class at the Unitarian Universalist Church of Fairfax. (UUCF.)

The sacredness of nature is a long-held theme in both the Unitarian and Universalist traditions, dating back to the writings of the New England transcendentalists. For some Unitarian Universalists, the sacred is best known and experienced in nature. Here members of the Paint Branch Unitarian Universalist Church in Adelphi, Maryland, gather for a service held outside in a natural setting. (PBUUC.)

Equal rights for women was an issue that concerned both Unitarians and Universalists in the 19th century. Representatives from both traditions were key figures in the campaign for women's suffrage, and many of the first American women ordained were Unitarians or Universalists. The tradition of exploring women's concerns and possibilities continues in this meeting of the Women's Center at Paint Branch Unitarian Universalist Church. (PBUUC.)

Unitarian Universalists from throughout the Washington area have continued the tradition of social witness. Many congregations have sent work crews to New Orleans to help that community recover from the devastating Hurricane Katrina of 2005. Crews provide hands-on help, cleaning and restoring houses for residents, making it possible for them to return to their homes. (ASC.)

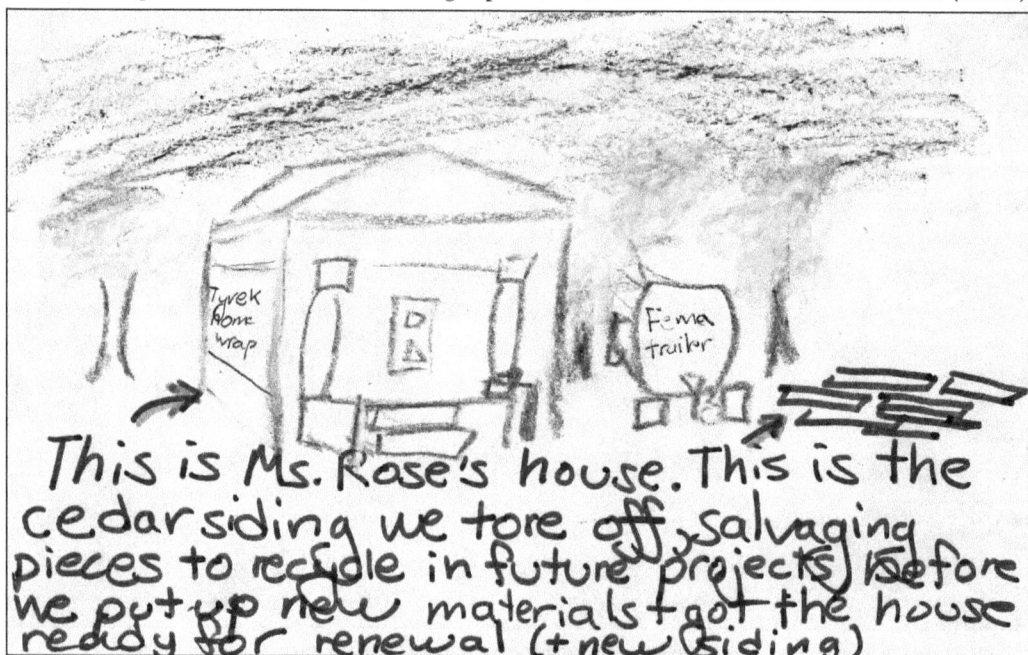

Tyvek Home wrap

Fema trailer

This is Ms. Rose's house. This is the cedar siding we tore off salvaging pieces to recycle in future projects before we put up new materials + got the house ready for renewal (+ new siding)

Those who went to New Orleans observed that they received as much from the experience as they contributed. This drawing by a participant notes the work they did. Another volunteer reported, "We spent most of the time laughing. I recovered from my office job. Worked hard too. Thought about community, inequality, and disaster relief." (ASC.)

David Eaton believed that "to be a Unitarian is to be a humanist," whether one's humanism draws from a theistic or non-theistic foundation. Therefore the church must be actively involved in causes that seek to improve the conditions in which people live. In this photograph, the All Souls Church delegation makes its way to a peace demonstration in New York's Central Park in 1982. (ASC.)

In 1822, Joseph Revere cast a bell for the First Unitarian Church of Washington. From the start, the bell was to have two purposes. It would be rung to summon the congregation to worship, and it was also to serve as a warning bell, alerting the population to dangers. That dual function continues to be honored as the bell approaches its 200th year. (ASC.)

113

An article in the *Washington Post* during the 1920s noted the "severe simplicity" of Unitarian worship. Today as Unitarian Universalists have sought to create more diverse congregations, they have experimented with forms of worship supporting that diversity. Music is an important way of expressing spirituality, and so a new diversity of song and performance is finding its way into Unitarian Universalist services. In 1977, Ysaye Barnwell, a member of Sweet Honey in the Rock, founded the Jubilee Singers at All Souls Church (pictured here). The current repertoire includes music from the African American tradition, world music, gospel, jazz, and blues, and the group performs not only at Sunday worship, but also as part of social outreach to senior citizens' facilities and community venues. Its statement of purpose declares, "We strive to be a diverse family of individuals that uses music as a vehicle to heal, encourage, and stimulate change while working toward a community and world that is more loving and just." (ASC.)

Eight

A COALITION OF RELIGIOUS LIBERALS

A. Powell Davies dreamed of a coalition of religious liberals joining to affirm its core values—religious freedom, social action, and a reasoned approach to faith. As the Unitarian Universalist presence in Washington approaches its 200th year, that dream is being realized, though perhaps in forms different from what Davies could have imagined.

Unitarian Universalist congregations in the Washington, D.C., region today offer a variety of options: religious humanism, liberal Christianity, and a world-religions-based faith. There are worship styles found in congregations that are reminiscent of the Protestant tradition, others that draw upon ethical humanism, and some that bring together a diverse variety of cultural references. Some congregations focus on religious education for children, some are social-action oriented, some draw from eastern religious traditions such as Buddhism, some have a special outreach to the gay and lesbian community, and some are intentional in seeking to create more diverse religious congregations. All Unitarian Universalist congregations in the Washington, D.C., area contain some combination of these elements and more.

In 1822, Robert Little, the first Unitarian minister in Washington, argued in a sermon given to the U.S. House of Representatives that people should have the right to follow their own reasoning and the lessons of their experience in matters of religious faith. In 1828, Theophilus Fiske gave the region's first Universalist sermon in Washington's city hall. He offered a view of a God whose primary message and desire for humankind was love. Throughout the years that have followed, Unitarians and Universalists—and Unitarian Universalists—have sought to create faith communities governed by these values.

As the forms of expression have changed throughout the years, the inherent wisdom of these traditions still speaks, offering opportunities for religious liberals to do their part in creating a more humane, more just, and more compassionate world.

UNIVERSALIST NATIONAL MEMORIAL CHURCH

Fiftieth Anniversary
of Services of Worship

Universalist National Memorial Church
Washington, D.C.

Washington, D.C.
April 20, 1980

In 1980, the Universalist National Memorial Church celebrated its 50th anniversary, marking a half-century in the nation's capital. Throughout those years, the church has been a worshipping community for liberal Christians. While affirming the Unitarian Universalist commitment to freedom of belief and a reasoned approach to faith, the church offers worship and service that is anchored in the Christian tradition. (UNMC.)

Universalists affirm that no soul is forever lost to God and that God's essential nature is love. A loving God would not exclude large segments of the world's population, and so Universalists recognize that Christianity is but one expression of humanity's yearning to be in relationship with the holy. Universalists seek to live and work together, honoring the many faces of God. This photograph is of the 1975 Christmas service. (UNMC.)

To articulate the faith that draws this congregation together, the Universalist National Memorial Church offers this mission statement: "We create a loving community for worship and service in the spirit of Jesus Christ. We welcome all and respect individual beliefs as we grow together." Pictured here is the congregation on Palm Sunday, 1991. (UNMC.)

The Unitarian Universalist Church of Silver Spring, originally the Silver Spring–Takoma Park Universalist Fellowship, was founded with support from the Universalist National Memorial Church. Here the two congregations celebrate their heritage with a shared worship service in the sanctuary of the Washington church. (Photograph by and courtesy of Bruce Marshall.)

The Ethical Culture Movement was founded in 1876 in New York City by Felix Adler, the son of a rabbi, who sought to create spiritual communities based not in religious creed but in the practice of ethical living. "Deed not creed" has been a guiding principle. Ethical societies emphasize a reasoned approach to religious questions and encourage members to become involved in efforts to create a more humane society, supporting such organizations as the American Civil Liberties Union, the Legal Aid Society, and the NAACP. The Washington Ethical Society was established in 1944. Members have been active in efforts to desegregate Washington, to end hunger and homelessness, and to extend the right of marriage to gay and lesbian couples. In 2008, the Washington Ethical Society affiliated with the Unitarian Universalist Association, in addition to its membership in the American Ethical Union. It now holds dual affiliation with the two national organizations. (WES.)

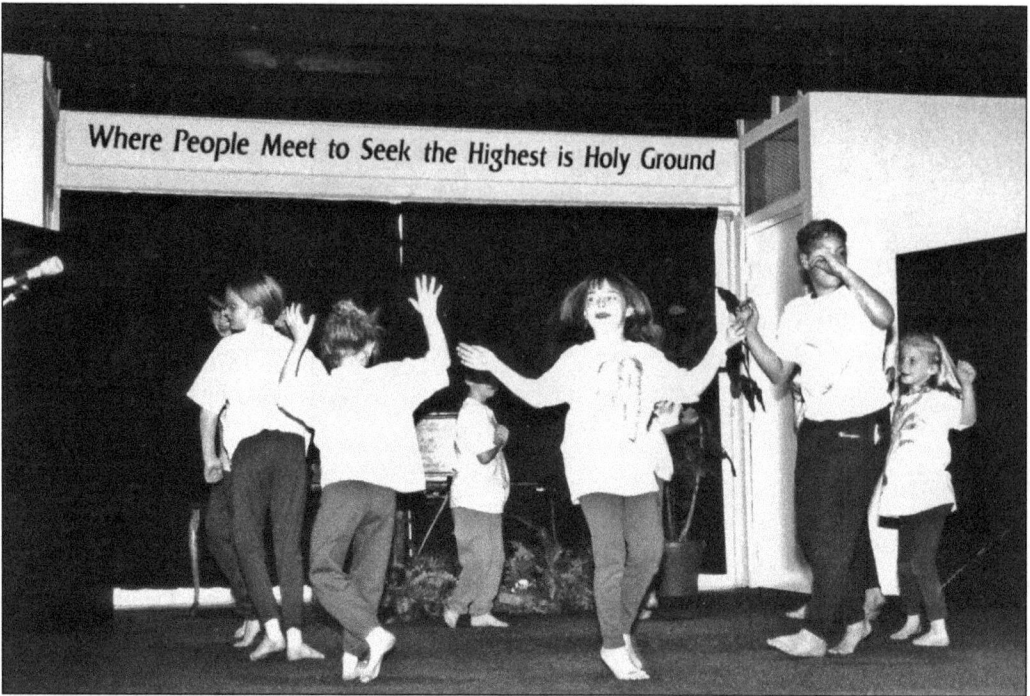

Where People Meet to Seek the Highest is Holy Ground

Ethical societies affirm a spirituality that conceives the highest purpose in life as helping create a more just and humane society. They affirm the worth and dignity of the individual and seek to bring out the best in each person. Members come together in community to celebrate life's joys and sorrows, and to help create a better world for this and subsequent generations. (WES.)

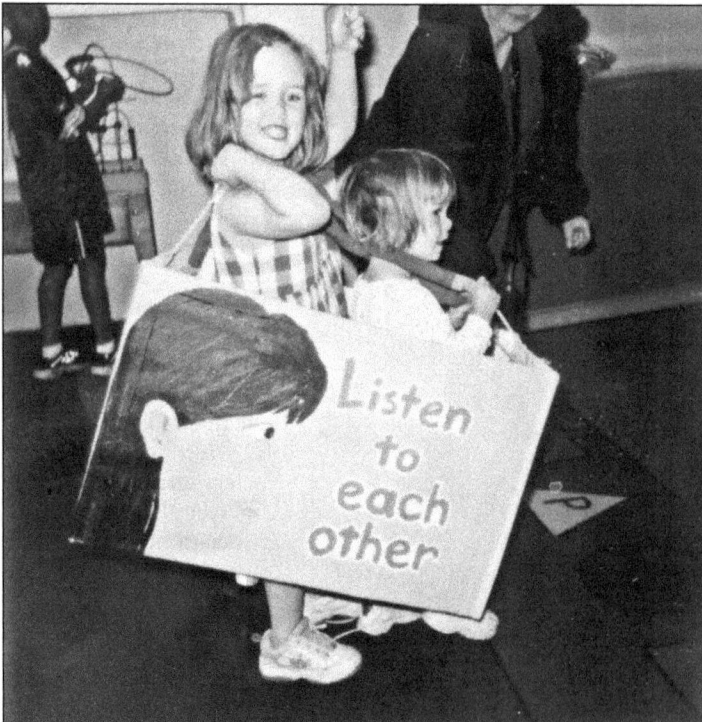

Listen to each other

Children's programs at the Washington Ethical Society aim "to teach children and teens to be kind and fair and to take responsibility for creating a better world." Children are helped to seek the best in themselves and others, as they are also encouraged to develop sustaining relationships and find their own way of making contributions to the larger society. (WES.)

In 1966, when the society planned to build its own facility, it sought to locate in a neighborhood that was integrated. A suitable site was found on Sixteenth Street in northwest Washington, and a building was constructed. This sign announces the commitment of the congregation to being an equal opportunity employer, that is, not to discriminate in employment because of race, religion, color, or national origin. (WES.)

The Washington Ethical Society was founded by people with a deep commitment to the civil rights movement. From that beginning, members have continued to be involved in actions for social change. This photograph is from the May 2000 Million Moms March, which sought more effective gun control. (WES.)

In this photograph, Unitarian Universalists gather in front of All Souls Church in Washington before participating in the March for Women's Lives, which was held on April 25, 2004. Reminiscent of the 1963 March on Washington for Jobs and Freedom, Unitarian Universalist participants came together from congregations throughout the Washington area, some sleeping on cots the night before at All Souls Church. Though the suburban Unitarian Universalist churches now show far greater membership than either of the founding congregations—Universalist National Memorial Church or All Souls Church—the Washington churches still serve as a centering presence for Unitarian Universalism throughout the metropolitan area. And from time to time, they offer opportunities for their progeny to come home. (ASC.)

The 2004 March for Women's Lives brought together women and men in support of the rights of women, including reproductive rights. It was intended as a "wake-up call" that the rights of women were being eroded and as a reminder that civil rights are protected only when individuals remain vigilant in the face of threats to liberties. (CLUUC.)

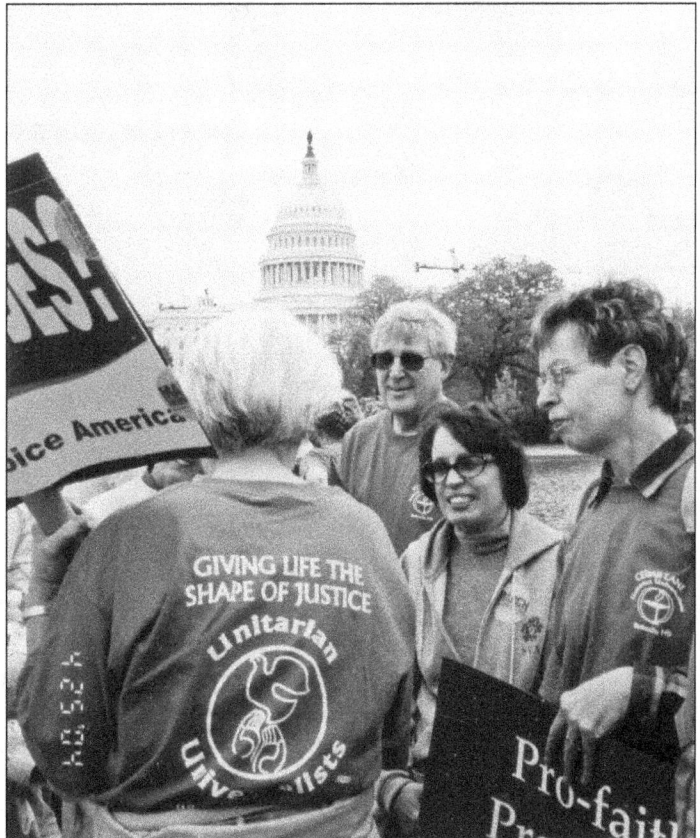

The dynamic between spiritual values and public witness has helped define Unitarian Universalism. What does it mean to be people of faith, living in a world in which there is often suffering and injustice? How can action in the public realm contribute to improving people's lives? (CLUUC.)

Opportunities for women as Unitarian and Universalist ministers have seen their ups and downs. Universalists and Unitarians were among the first American denominations to ordain women in the mid-19th century, but jobs in churches were not plentiful. Today, however, Unitarian Universalists show the highest percentage of women serving as clergy among American denominations. Pictured here is Shana Lynngood, associate minister of All Souls Church. (ASC.)

Unitarian Universalist congregations have been strong supporters of human rights for gay, lesbian, bisexual, and transgender people. Churches have offered their facilities for support groups, classes, and coffee houses. Many congregation members and ministers are openly gay. And the Unitarian Universalist Association has organized support for the right of gay people to marry. Pictured here is a delegation from River Road Unitarian Universalist Congregation. (RRUUC.)

At the center of Unitarian Universalism is the congregation: those who freely choose to form a religious community grounded in ideals of human worth and dignity, the free search for religious truth, and a spirituality that unites people of different heritages and beliefs. Unitarian Universalist congregations are democratically governed, with the national Unitarian Universalist Association existing to support local congregations, not rule them. (ASC.)

After attending the Unitarian Universalist General Assembly, a new member of the Universalist National Memorial Church wrote, "What holds the Unitarian Universalist movement together is the common belief in love and acceptance wherever, and however, that might be found . . . Our movement makes an affirmative effort to create a space in which people are loved and accepted." Pictured from left to right are All Souls Church members Saundra Assante, Herbert Woods, and Elizabeth King. (ASC.)

Programs for children in liberal churches found their voice in the 1930s as curricula were developed that focused on building character rather than memorizing Bible verses or creedal formulas. That emphasis continues today as children in Unitarian Universalist congregations are encouraged to develop their identities as religious and ethical people: what they care about, what they stand for, who they aspire to be. (ASC.)

Observing an ancient tradition, the senior minister of All Souls Church, Rob Hardies, welcomes a child into the congregation. For almost 200 years, Unitarians and Universalists have represented the values and affirmations of religious liberalism in the Washington, D.C., area. The tradition continues as new generations now step up to assume their roles in this continuing story. (ASC.)

BIBLIOGRAPHY

Bordewich, Fergus M. *Washington: The Making of the American Capital*. New York: HarperCollins, 2008.

Brooks, Seth R. *The Issues of Life*. Washington, D.C.: Universalist National Memorial Church, 1985.

Davies, A. Powell. *The Language of the Heart*. Washington, D.C.: A. Powell Davies Memorial Committee, 1956.

History Book Committee, Cedar Lane Unitarian Universalist Church. *Cedar Lane Unitarian Universalist Church: The First Fifty Years*. Bethesda, MD: Cedar Lane Unitarian Universalist Church, 2001.

Holmes, David L. *The Faiths of the Founding Fathers*. New York: Oxford University Press, 2006.

Howe, Charles A. *The Larger Faith: A Short History of American Universalism*. Boston: Skinner House Books, 1993.

Howlett, Duncan. *No Greater Love: The James Reeb Story*. Boston: Skinner House Books, 1993.

Miller, Russell E. *The Larger Hope: The First Century of Universalism in America*. Boston: Unitarian Universalist Association, 1986.

Miller, Russell E. *The Larger Hope: The Second Century of Universalism in America* Boston: Unitarian Universalist Association, 1986.

Perman, Dagmar Horna. *The Gerard Street Project*. Washington, D.C.: All Souls Church, Unitarian, 1964.

Scudder, Jennie W. *A Century of Unitarianism in the National Capital*. Boston: Beacon Press, 1922.

Staples, Laurence C. *Washington Unitarianism*. Washington, D.C.: All Souls Church, Unitarian, 1970.

Unitarian Universalist Historical Society. *Dictionary of Unitarian and Universalist Biography*. http://www25.uua.org/uuhs/duub.

Van Schaik, Jr., John. *Historical Sermon*. Archives of the Universalist National Memorial Church, 1904.

Zenzen, Joan M. *A History of River Road Unitarian Church: In Commemoration of its Fortieth Anniversary*. Bethesda, MD: River Road Unitarian Church, 1999.

Visit us at
arcadiapublishing.com